Benches in the Bathroom

Leading a Physically, Emotionally, and Socially Safe School Culture

EVISHA FORD

Solution Tree | Press

Copyright © 2023 by Solution Tree Press

Materials appearing here are copyrighted. With one exception, all rights are reserved. Readers may reproduce only those pages marked "Reproducible." Otherwise, no part of this book may be reproduced or transmitted in any form or by any means (electronic, photocopying, recording, or otherwise) without prior written permission of the publisher.

555 North Morton Street
Bloomington, IN 47404
800.733.6786 (toll free) / 812.336.7700
FAX: 812.336.7790

email: info@SolutionTree.com
SolutionTree.com

Visit go.SolutionTree.com/educatorwellness to download the free reproducibles in this book.

Printed in the United States of America

Library of Congress Cataloging-in-Publication Data

Names: Ford, Evisha, author.
Title: Benches in the bathroom : leading a physically, emotionally, and
   socially safe school culture / Evisha Ford.
Description: Bloomington, IN : Solution Tree Press, [2023] | Includes
   bibliographical references and index.
Identifiers: LCCN 2022055898 (print) | LCCN 2022055899 (ebook) | ISBN
   9781954631557 (paperback) | ISBN 9781954631564 (ebook)
Subjects: LCSH: Teachers--Job stress--Prevention. | Teachers--Psychology. |
   Teaching--Psychological aspects. | Burn out (Psychology) | Health
   promotion. | Teachers--Conduct of life. | Teachers--Job satisfaction.
Classification: LCC LB2840.2 .F67 2023 (print) | LCC LB2840.2 (ebook) |
   DDC 371.1001/9--dc23/eng/20230301
LC record available at https://lccn.loc.gov/2022055898
LC ebook record available at https://lccn.loc.gov/2022055899

Solution Tree
Jeffrey C. Jones, CEO
Edmund M. Ackerman, President

Solution Tree Press
President and Publisher: Douglas M. Rife
Associate Publishers: Kendra Slayton and Todd Brakke
Editorial Director: Laurel Hecker
Art Director: Rian Anderson
Copy Chief: Jessi Finn
Production Editor: Kate St. Ives
Copy Editor: Evie Madsen
Proofreader: Mark Hain
Text and Cover Designer: Laura Cox
Acquisitions Editor: Hilary Goff
Assistant Acquisitions Editor: Elijah Oates
Content Development Specialist: Amy Rubenstein
Associate Editor: Sarah Ludwig
Editorial Assistant: Anne Marie Watkins

Acknowledgments

Writing this book was an endeavor more demanding than I could have imagined. I am grateful to God for the vision and provision. I am blessed by the people who cheered for me on this journey.

My mother maintains her status as my chief encouragement officer. My love, and self-proclaimed "biggest fan," kept the vision of this completed project in focus for me when it was blurry. I am grateful for my little boys, who graciously forwent my attention on countless evenings and weekends, and for my family, sister-friends, and colleagues who had faith in me from the inception of this project, when it was only a vague concept.

Thank you, Kristen, for your enthusiasm about this topic from the beginning; this would have been a completely different book without you! I appreciate the entire Solution Tree team for its confidence in this work; the incredible and layered support has been amazing.

I am grateful for my iCan Dream Center family—the best of the best in catapulting learners to success. My confidence in your love for our students provided the mental clarity and space for this undertaking.

Solution Tree Press would like to thank the following reviewers:

Heather Bell-Williams
Principal, Milltown
　Elementary School
Anglophone South School District
St. Stephen, New Brunswick, Canada

Doug Crowley
Assistant Principal
DeForest Area High School
DeForest, Wisconsin

Abbey Duggins
Assistant Superintendent
Saluda County Schools
Saluda, South Carolina

Kelly Hilliard
Math Teacher
McQueen High School
Reno, Nevada

Karen Johnson
Coordinator of Language Acquisition
Pleasanton Unified School District
Pleasanton, California

Jed Kees
Principal
Onalaska Middle School
Onalaska, Wisconsin

Ian Landy
Principal
School District 47 (Powell River)
Powell River, British Columbia, Canada

Louis Lim
Vice Principal
Bayview Secondary School
Richmond Hill, Ontario, Canada

Peter Marshall
Education Consultant
Burlington, Ontario, Canada

Rosalind Poon
Vice Principal 8–12
Richmond School District
Richmond, British Columbia, Canada

Katie Saunders
Middle School Teacher
Anglophone School District West
Woodstock, New Brunswick, Canada

Steven Weber
Associate Superintendent for Teaching and Learning
Fayetteville Public Schools
Fayetteville, Arkansas

Visit **go.SolutionTree.com/educatorwellness** to download the free reproducibles in this book.

Table of Contents

Reproducibles are in italics.

About the Author vii

Introduction 1
    About This Book 5

1 Cultures of Wellness 9
    The Impact of Organizational Climate and Culture 10
    Elements of Organizational Culture in Your School 11
    What a Well School Culture Is *Not* 15
    What a Well School Culture Is 16
    The Culture Within 18

2 Pain Points 21
    Foundational Knowledge About Trauma 23
    Toxic Stress as a Form of Trauma 28
    The Culture Within 33
    Burnout Risk Scale 36
    Leadership ACEs Survey 38

3 Trauma-Informed Compassion 41
    Trauma-Informed Care and Its Contribution to Effective Leadership . . . 42
    From Trauma Informed to Trauma Compassionate 47
    The Trauma-Compassionate Approach and the Framework for a
       Culture of Wellness 47
    The Organization as Family 48
    The Culture Within 52
    Traditions and Celebrations Planning Tool 55

4 People-First Leadership 57
    Philosophies of People-First Leadership 59
    People-First Leadership and the Framework for a Culture of Wellness . . . 65

  The Culture Within 68
  SWOP Analysis 71

5 Team Leadership 73
  Create Connection 75
  Be Present 77
  Check In First 77
  Create Structure 79
  Build Community 80
  Utilize Think Time and Processing Time 81
  Infuse Choice 83
  Guard Emotional Safety 83
  Respect Time Away 86
  Pay It Forward 87
  The Culture Within 90
  Meeting Agenda Planner 93
  RACI Board 94

6 Organizational Leadership 95
  Fear of Change 96
  Identify Toxicity Within an Organization 98
  Create Space for the Human Experience 100
  Hire for Zeal 102
  Encourage Vacations 104
  Include Wellness in Collective Bargaining 107
  Give Staff Permission to Engage in Self-Care 109
  The Culture Within 112
  Hire for Zeal Interview Questions 115
  Wellness Initiative Planning Checklist 117

7 A Journey to Wellness 119
  Working and Learning in Paradise 120
  Strategies for Cultural Wellness at Paradise 123
  The Culture Within 131

Epilogue 135
  Modeling Self-Care as a Critical Action in Leading a Physically, Emotionally, and Socially Safe School Culture 137

References and Resources 139

Index 151

About the Author

Evisha Ford, EdD, is founding executive director of the iCan Dream Center (https://icandreamcenter.com), a therapeutic school in Illinois that serves the needs of neurodiverse learners and their families. Dr. Ford began her career working with inner-city homeless youth in Chicago, providing therapeutic intervention and linkages to community resources. She partnered with various community agencies to build their capacity to support the needs of vulnerable youth via training, resource development, and program evaluation. Chicago Public Schools recruited Dr. Ford, which launched her path in education. She is a former assistant superintendent, director of special education, and assistant professor of educational leadership.

Dr. Ford is a sought-after thought leader and consultant for social-impact organizations across the United States and internationally. She specializes in trauma-compassionate leadership, program design, cultural and racial equity, developing continuums of service for diverse learners, and a variety of other topics relevant to effective school and nonprofit leadership.

Additionally, Dr. Ford serves as president of the board for the United Way Blue Island Robbins Neighborhood Network. In March 2018, Zeta Phi Beta Sorority named Dr. Ford Woman of the Year. In July 2018, she was honored as one of the influential 100 Black Women in Chicago for her educational contributions. In the winter of 2019, she received the Paige Award for her impact in the special needs community. In July 2019, the Professional Women's Network recognized her as a community igniter. In July 2022, she received the Dream Maker Award from the Bronzeville Children's Museum of Chicago. Dr. Ford's most significant and generous award came from her two sons, Nolan and Josiah, who have repeatedly named her "best mom ever."

Dr. Ford's passion for marginalized youth began at an early age. She earned a master's degree in social work from the University of Illinois Urbana-Champaign and completed doctoral studies in educational leadership at Aurora University in 2010. Her research focus was students with disabilities, youth resilience, and systemic injustice.

To learn more about Dr. Ford's work, visit her website (http://drevisha.com) or follow her on LinkedIn at DrEvishaFord.

To book Evisha Ford for professional development, contact pd@solutiontree.com.

Introduction

Benches in the bathrooms are an antidote for teacher burnout.

It sounds like a ridiculous statement, doesn't it? Depending on the environment you work in, you may or may not be used to the idea of bathrooms having benches at all. But when I was the assistant superintendent in a public school district, I gave a board member a tour of our newly renovated elementary school. We reached one of the women's restrooms and walked inside. She looked around briefly and asked, "Where are the benches?"

I glanced around the room. Toilets? Check. Sinks? Check. Soap dispensers? Running water? Mirrors? TP? Checks all around. Benches? No check.

The board member saw the confusion on my face. She explained, "Yes. The benches—where teachers can go to cry."

After that conversation, I did some thinking about what the board member had said, and I had one of those *aha moments*. There are very few private spaces in most work environments, especially in schools. Even fewer are those secret places where a teacher can let off some steam and stress of the day. Yes, life is hard, and sometimes we must cry. I realized that if there hadn't been another option for me (that is, my supervisor's sofa), I'd have spent some time myself on the benches that my district eventually added to the restrooms.

It's no wonder educators are stressed. In addition to asking them to teach, influence, and guide students toward a successful future, leaders also ask educators to steer students through the social and emotional upheavals of growing up. And sadly, in some cases, this also means navigating trauma, including domestic violence, abuse, poverty, and neglect, to name only a few of the environments in which many students live. Educational administrators and teachers see all of it.

Like most who dedicate their lives to others via social services professions, many teachers emotionally invest in their students, and this investment takes a great deal of energy; it's taxing.

In addition to the stress that results from witnessing the traumas students may face and helping to guide them academically, emotionally, and socially—often with the lived experience of trauma—educators, and teachers especially, must contend with day-to-day logistic responsibilities that make their profession demanding. These responsibilities include preparing lessons, grading, testing, and meeting accountability requirements, to name a few. If you add a lack of administrative support to this mix, along with extra duties—too much parent involvement, too little parent involvement, and the necessity of addressing individual and unique student needs—the job becomes even more stressful. Do you now or have you ever felt overworked? (Yes, that's a rhetorical question.) Overwork seems to be so ingrained in the field of education that it's a part of the culture in many organizations. It's culturally acceptable, perhaps interpreted as a badge of honor. In some places, administrators might even expect it.

The presence of existing adult trauma compounds the stress of witnessing students' trauma and the routine demands of the teaching profession. That's right, people's private lives don't cease to exist when they walk into work. The stress that stems from trauma educators may have experienced themselves (past or present) affects how they interact with one another and their students. It affects the energy they have, what kind of support they need, and how they function. Ultimately, it affects students and the quality of the care and guidance they receive in school.

The consequences of stress in an educational setting vary and are often severe for the educators themselves and their students. The consequences for teachers include diminished productivity stemming from high daily stress, burnout that may lead to leaving the profession early, and reduced student outcomes. Consider the following.

- Forty-six percent of teachers in the United States report high daily stress during the school year (Niroga Institute, 2021).
- Many teachers who leave the profession do so before retirement age (Loewus, 2021).
- Teachers' stress leads to a lessened ability to offer high-quality instruction and the behavior supports students may need, resulting in lower academic achievement and increased disruptive behaviors in students (Herman, Hickmon-Rosa, & Reinke, 2018).

What's more, the credentialing process for administrators and teachers focuses on pedagogy, compliance, and preparation for instructional leadership. As an assistant professor, I was tasked with developing and aligning graduate course work for national accreditation. There were no requirements for the inclusion of stress-coping strategies for educational practitioners. Educators can anticipate spending their entire teaching careers (however long those careers last) with no formal training to help them manage the inevitable stress and trauma that come with this profession. It's no wonder teachers experience burnout and compassion fatigue, and eventually retire early, quit, or suffer through the workday or school year.

Lack of training, guidance, and support contributes to a crisis of teacher attrition and turnover in schools, resulting in a disservice to students. In a worldwide study on factors that influence teacher retention, researchers discovered that teacher attrition rates are as high as 50 percent in the first five years of teaching (Gunn & McRae, 2021). The same study notes, "Healthy and supportive professional working environments that value new teacher contributions and honor the notion of personal health and well-being in and out of the classroom are crucial" (Gunn & McRae, 2021). This kind of support creates a climate and culture that permit teachers to thrive in their instructional environment and career (Beck & Servage, 2018).

I entered my first leadership role almost by accident. After completing my leadership credentials, I was being mentored for leadership in a department in desperate need of an overhaul when the director's wife suddenly became quite ill. For three months, I assumed additional responsibilities so the director could tend to his wife's needs. One day I arrived at work to find a note with his passwords and a message stating, "Not sure when I will return." He never returned fully, and at age twenty-seven, I became the director of special education. This appointment came just in time for the state to take notice of the antiquated practices in the department, which positioned me to lead substantial changes (that is, addressing placement options for students with disabilities and the integration of these students in the less-restrictive learning environments of their typically developing peers).

During my tenure, I created or overhauled five programs. I got into the rhythm of staffing, designing physical learning spaces, and identifying curriculum. After the state dismissed the district from their oversight, I continued to innovate on behalf of vulnerable students. At one point, I noticed a gap for students and created yet another program design. The superintendent did not see the need for the program, nor did he approve it; I left the school district at the end of that year.

I used the program design the superintendent rejected as a blueprint and founded a nonprofit organization dedicated to addressing the needs of marginalized youth. I went on to become an assistant professor and department program leader.

I contributed to the development of two graduate programs for school leaders and thoroughly enjoyed mentoring educators who were hopeful for school-leadership roles. Simultaneously, I poured my knowledge and experience into fine-tuning my nonprofit. Later, I served as an assistant superintendent; I spent five years in that role before I made my departure from leadership in public education to focus my efforts on the nonprofit I founded, the iCan Dream Center (https://icandreamcenter.com).

The *iCan Dream Center* is a school serving neurodiverse learners almost exclusively. Initially, it served high school and postsecondary learners, but in year seven, I expanded the center to serve early childhood students, preK through third graders. The iCan Dream Center went from a small but mighty team of four serving a couple dozen students to a team of over fifty, with an enrollment of one hundred learners and a daunting and growing waiting list. My staff has survived growing pains, teacher shortages, and tragedy, in part, because of a deliberate culture of wellness. The iCan Dream Center educator-turnover rate defies all the research about therapeutic school environments, which can be particularly stressful and ripe for burnout (Hemati & Moradi, 2021).

This book is for K–12 school and district leaders. I leverage research-backed theory and strategies along with my own experiences, particularly those experiences of starting a nonprofit school dedicated to therapeutic efforts, to offer a guide for leaders to mitigate the impact of stress on the educators they serve. Most future leaders enter the field (and subsequently leadership) with confidence they can make a positive impact. Their greatest opportunity to do so might be in reducing the chaos to clear a path for better instruction and targeted student services. Effective leaders take a *universal design approach* (that is, an approach that seeks to ensure everyone is successful) and front-load the work environment with supports that allow *all* teachers to thrive regardless of the nature of their personal experiences or the traumas in their backgrounds.

Educators cannot take the stress and trauma out of the school environment. That's here to stay. So yes, sometimes they must find a bench or sofa, supply closet, or that spot under a tree or the steps out back, and cry. It's good to have these spaces—more so if a caring leader designates them as private, safe spaces. However, educators need more than benches in the bathroom where they can go to release tension, stress, and frustrations; they need to create environments that reduce the need for the benches. Leaders need to develop a culture in schools that nurtures its members with empathy, sustained support, and opportunities for growth. Leaders need to develop a schoolwide culture of wellness. I wrote this book to help school and district leaders do just that.

About This Book

Wellness and self-care are vital for all educators to help combat the stress and chaos at work (and in their personal lives). There are many excellent books on self-care for educators that promote individual well-being and guide them toward establishing healthy wellness habits. While this book touches on educator self-care and the development of healthy habits, its focus is to help K–12 educational leaders (superintendents, assistant superintendents, principals, assistant principals, and all others who lead, whether at the district, school, or department level in a variety of leadership roles) establish a culture of wellness as a critical step in combating teacher burnout and attrition. Educational leaders are well positioned to engineer a culture of wellness within their departments and schools because they set the tone by modeling, influencing, and establishing the behavioral expectations of the individuals they serve. A leader who's committed and focused on establishing and maintaining a safe, comfortable working culture for others will find answers here. By integrating information on trauma-informed care, compassion, and authentic leadership, and by using the team- and organization-level strategies in the later chapters, educational leaders can transform the culture of their school or district. The steps to transformation are small, and the changes take time, but they lead to a culture where teachers feel valued, healthy, happy, safe, and successful at work. This ensures teachers will stay the course and continue to dedicate themselves to students who need them.

I've divided this book into seven chapters and an epilogue. The book's narrative arc moves from a broad examination of organizational culture and what a well culture is, to an in-depth look at the role stress plays in toxic cultures. It offers a culture-building framework for leadership and specific strategies to use at the team and organization levels. It also offers a real-life example of a principal implementing and sustaining a culture of wellness. It is best to read the book from beginning to end to derive the most value; however, it is also possible to work through the content in any order that suits your needs. Following is a description of each chapter.

Chapter 1 defines organizational culture and the impact that culture has on the performance of its members. It details the factors that influence culture within a K–12 education context. It looks closely at what a culture of wellness in schools is not, then clarifies what it is, and offers a framework to guide the development of a well culture through the integration of the key contributing modes I examine in this book. Finally, it examines sustainability and the critical behaviors for sustaining a school culture of wellness.

Chapter 2 explores the nature of the work environment as a source of toxic stress and identifies some of those sources of stress, such as racism, abusive leadership, bullying (including cyberbullying), sexual harassment, and boundary issues. The chapter shows how repeated and harmful occurrences can trigger further stress in those most vulnerable due to previous life experiences, and how this compounded stress impacts and impairs how and what teachers and administrators do.

Chapter 3 introduces the concept of trauma-informed care as a foundation for proactive extension and trauma-compassionate leadership. You will learn how this approach transforms the work environment to one that acts and feels more like a high-functioning family, where the individual is valued over numbers and checked boxes, which is all too prevalent in many schools.

Chapter 4 encompasses the importance of developing a leadership philosophy and offers two philosophy-backed leadership styles: (1) servant and (2) transformational. Both styles have aspects grounded in serving and empowering others, attributes vital to positive culture shifts. Together they inform a people-first approach.

Chapter 5 features strategies for change at the team or department level—that is, the places where suboptimal team conditions may exist and where leaders have more influence over those conditions than they might at an organizational level.

Chapter 6 contains organizational strategies that expand ideas on how leaders can further create a culture of wellness in an entire organization. This involves institutionalizing a culture so wellness is embedded in the fiber of the organization, not just experienced in well-led pockets. Changes at the organizational level may appear especially daunting and even impossible, but moving beyond behaviors that indicate a paralyzing fear of change can move organizations beyond what leaders think is possible. Organizational strategies focus on changing culture by reducing or preventing stress and chaos in the school's systems. These strategies are at the heart of designing a culture of wellness within an educational organization.

Chapter 7 presents an example of a real high-functioning, healthy culture by introducing a middle school where the leader purposefully applied strategies for cultural change you'll find in this book. The middle school created and has sustained a positive environment. The resulting culture has retained thriving teachers—without attrition—for over a decade.

In addition to the information and strategies, each of the first six chapters opens with a relatable story of educator stress and the factors that contributed to that stress. (While each of these stories is based on a real-life situation, I have changed names and minor circumstantial details.) Each chapter closes with an interactive element called *The Culture Within*. This element invites readers to synthesize the book's content through an examination of their own thoughts, values, and perceptions that guide their outward behaviors as school and district leaders, because leader-led systemic culture change often starts with leader reflection and mindset change. Explore The Culture Within sections and activities as a group activity (such as a book study) or reflect on them individually. Some chapters also offer separate reproducible tools that allow readers to build on chapter content.

Regardless of the size or type of your school or organization, you can bring about culture change because it's the leadership—including *you*—not the structure or function of the school that creates, transforms, and sustains organizational culture. School principals are in a position to influence the daily experience of the educators in their building. Department heads can positively affect the practitioners on their team. Central office administrators and leaders of social-impact organizations can alter the fabric of the organization and the systems within, resulting in critical and positive impact. Using the team and organizational strategies you will find in this book, you will, over time, instill trust through transparency and engage (or re-engage) teachers with their purpose to inspire an environment of wellness to benefit all who enter it.

If you are reading this book, you care enough to be an effective, successful leader. I *love* that! The world needs more people like you—people who are dedicated to making an impact in the world. I wrote this book for you. The work ahead may seem larger than your current capacity. However, I assure you this is doable, and I will shine a light on your path. So, turn the page and let's get going.

CHAPTER 1

Cultures of Wellness

Not everything that weighs you down is yours to carry.
—Anonymous

In late spring of 2020, Kim, a teacher colleague, contacted me out of the blue about work-related stresses she was experiencing. Kim, who taught with all her heart and soul, sounded distraught and conflicted and needed to talk to someone about it. She couldn't speak to anyone at her workplace. I simply asked her, "What do you want to do?" Despite her conflicted feelings, she replied with finality, "Leave public education entirely." Our conversation revealed Kim was exhausted, disengaged, and depressed. Her students and her personal life were suffering because of this. She concluded by telling me her school environment was toxic.

Yep, *toxic* was the word she used. It wasn't the pay, the long hours, or misbehaving students. It was the toxic environment. Kim had been a credentialed teacher for more than ten years and had planned on teaching until she retired, but her school environment was so stressful she decided to leave midcareer.

I suspect many educators out there are just like Kim—exceptional, devoted, and experienced—halfway through their careers and feeling unable to continue their work. Why? Because they can't find *a bench in the bathroom*, nor do they have any confidence they will find an educational work environment where they don't need a bench to retreat to. Kim left teaching to help herself in a way she could not achieve in her workplace. What caused her to leave is what educators commonly refer to as *burnout*.

Kim leaving education was "the icing on my already-baked cake" that prodded me to action. I had grown tired of witnessing good educators leave the field due to preventable anguish. That year, I was fortunate to hire a few excellent educators at the iCan Dream Center who needed a soft place to land after feeling beat up. This narrative was becoming too familiar. The state board of education then commissioned me to develop a full-day workshop on cultures of wellness for school leaders; however, I wavered on moving forward due to the time commitment. Kim's story was the nudge I needed to remind me that students' lives were hanging in the balance. I asked myself, "How can leaders inspire a culture of wellness and self-care using their position and expertise to reduce the stress and chaos that causes burnout?" Ultimately, much of my research to answer that question for the workshop I translated into this book.

When I first asked myself how leaders could inspire a culture of wellness and self-care, I felt the enormity of what they would have to do. It was like the proverbial elephant in the room with me—maybe even an entire herd! Thinking about implementing cultural change in an organization can feel daunting. Leaders must first take the courageous step of self-reflection and own their contribution to less-than-ideal school environments to implement the necessary changes. However, articulating that step, how to do it, and what following steps to take can be an enormous task. The study of organizational climate and culture provide some sense of how to clarify where to start.

The Impact of Organizational Climate and Culture

When people think of an organization's culture, they likely tend to picture aspects of its climate. The *climate* of an organization denotes what people feel about an organization or how they feel in it, that is, "the sense, feeling or atmosphere people get in the organisation on either a day-to-day basis or just generally" (Wilkinson, n.d.). However, an organization's *culture* tends to encompass much beyond casual human awareness. There is no single definition of organizational culture. Preeminent scholar on organizational culture Edgar H. Schein (1985) describes *culture* as a group's shared assumptions that they develop and use as they adapt to external challenges and integrate experiences of confronting those challenges internally. The Society for Human Resource Management (SHRM; 2016) says *organizational culture* is "the glue that keeps an organization together. It is the silent code of conduct; it's more about how things get done, rather than what gets done."

So an organization's shared values and beliefs dictate what its employees are going to say, do, and feel about how the work gets done. When the climate or environment staff experience is deeply negative (as in Kim's story), students are the ones who bear the brunt. Even when teachers decide to remain in the system, it is difficult (if not impossible) for them to thrive professionally. When teachers don't have the bandwidth to pursue ideas, implement strategies, or even show up emotionally, students are at a disadvantage.

Ask yourself, "Is my school climate positive, and is my school culture healthy?" Though largely unseen, a school's culture—its professed and often unspoken values—has a significant impact on how staff behave, think, and treat others. In short, organizational culture impacts the success of all teaching and learning efforts that occur within a school. Kent D. Peterson (2002), educational consultant and professor emeritus at the University of Wisconsin–Madison, defines *school culture* as "the set of norms, values and beliefs, rituals and ceremonies, symbols and stories that make up the 'persona' of the school" (p. 10).

Leaders of any organization are vital to the introduction, development, and sustainability of the culture—good or bad. Regardless of the intentions of its leaders (and the leaders who follow), what behaviors ultimately occur and persist within the organization will either redefine or sustain the culture over time. In ideal cases, the culture is encouraging, safe, and supportive. In other cases, it is every bit as toxic as what Kim experienced, and that toxicity is felt by a group's members every day. So how do leaders expose and address those often-unseen components—the elements of culture that affect a workplace's climate and the well-being of its members?

Elements of Organizational Culture in Your School

While the elements of culture contributing to your team, school, or district's climate will take some work to discover, getting a reading on the atmosphere is a great starting point for identifying culture, and an early step in working to develop a culture of wellness. Think of this atmospheric quality as your organization's "heartbeat," the elements of its atmosphere that are palpable, that can be felt, and give activities in the organization a certain rhythm. Every organization has a heartbeat: department stores, gas stations, museums, banks, and yes, schools. Your school has a culture, and this culture has a heartbeat. Can you describe this heartbeat? Can you feel it? More importantly, how do your teachers, students, and staff perceive the heartbeat?

Distributing an anonymous climate survey is one way to get a sense of how your teachers, students, and staff experience the school environment. The U.S. Department of Education (n.d.) developed a free survey to assess the perspective of various stakeholders. The anonymity of the survey is important as it will yield more authentic responses, particularly in an environment that may feel unsafe.

Some questions I adapted from the survey that may be beneficial as a starting point are as follows. How would your teachers answer each question on a scale of 1–10?

- This school emphasizes showing respect for all cultural beliefs and practices. Do you feel like you belong?
- Relational aggression and harassment can be frequent problems at school. Do you feel safe physically, socially, and emotionally?
- This school would like to make implementing proactive strategies to manage student and staff stress levels a priority. Do you feel safeguards are in place to mitigate your stress?

The act of gathering insight from your team members is one way to show that you value their experiences and input in determining the path to a culture of wellness. Additionally, your team members' answers to your survey questions will show you trends in perception in your organization's culture and allow you to prioritize as you plan changes or make further inquiries. Culture isn't necessarily something on the lobby walls or that you include in your mission and vision statements and annual reports. However, you may find some clues to culture in the core values and the condition of the school walls and what adorns them.

Organizational culture is distinct to each institution. The culture in one school is different from that in another school because of the people who work there; the community in which the school exists, the leaders, teachers, and support staff are also unique and express the culture in many different ways. What are the underlying attitudes and influences within your school? What traditions do you celebrate? What do your staff meetings look and feel like? Is there joy in the atmosphere?

Take a school's dress code, for example. When was the last time you walked the halls outside parent-teacher conferences and saw dresses and ties? How would you feel if you walked into a school today and saw teachers and administrators wearing suits, ties, skirts, and heels? That was a different culture from another time, but seeing it now would speak loudly about the culture of that school, wouldn't it?

In many school environments, teachers come to school dressed comfortably and relaxed. Teachers, service providers, and administrators wear more casual clothes and often sport special holiday attire. You've seen it: costumes, pumpkin earrings, that sort of thing. Seasonal attire is a part of school culture. I admit I used to cringe when I saw it. Now, however, I've come to embrace it and even participate! Yes, dress codes can be a subtle but influential part of an organization's culture.

Another subtle but critical component of culture is work expectations. In addition to the approximately six hours a day a teacher spends in a classroom with students, there's additional time they need for preparation and planning, email and communications, grading, professional development, and extra duties that arise, like lunch duty or heading up a special program or curricular project. Do your teachers have ample time during the school day to get the work done? Or do you expect teachers to take work home to complete during the evenings and weekends?

Regardless of what the organization's culture looks like, and regardless of whether the organization is a high school, elementary school, charter school, private school, or an alternative or therapeutic school, the following two concepts are resolute.

1. The behaviors and attitudes staff demonstrate come from the top (that's you, the leader) and trickle down—*always*. It's educational leaders who have both the ability and, more importantly, the responsibility to foster a culture of wellness teachers so desperately need in education.

2. Individual coping is important in creating a positive school climate; however, most critical to sustainability is a comprehensive and schoolwide commitment (National Education Association, 2018).

Employing that one educator—that one shining star, who is by nature resilient enough to cope with workplace stress is great. Leaders need to find as many of those teachers as they can. However, as an educational leader, your job is to reduce and eliminate the toxicity in the environment so *all* teachers can thrive and shine brightly.

What are some specific attributes to look for when assessing the culture in your own school? What would those attributes look like when functioning in a way that is supportive (rather than deleterious) to members of the school community? Terrence E. Deal, the Irving R. Melbo professor at the University of Southern California Rossier School, and Kent D. Peterson (2016) offer a list of these attributes that includes norms, values and beliefs, rituals and ceremonies, and symbols and stories that I embrace and expand on in this book.

Norms

Norms are a compilation of an organization's values, beliefs, and rituals. They serve as a guide to language, thinking, behavior, and interactions members expect in a social group. Positive, supportive norms in a school might include the following, which are applicable to all educators in the school.

- Be willing to take on responsibilities.
- Feel a sense of responsibility for student learning.
- Be conscious of costs and resources use.

- Speak with pride about the school and your team.
- Share useful information and new ideas.
- Tell stories that recognize the contributions of others.
- Work hard and have fun. (Deal & Peterson, 2016)

Values and Beliefs

According to Deal and Peterson (2016), *values* dictate the school's priorities while *beliefs* guide how people interact with their environment and often hinge on faith rather than evidence. An example of a belief at the iCan Dream Center is that students perform better when the community of educators connect with and address the critical needs of families. The organization values its parent coach enough to prioritize her salary in the budget. She meets with the family of each enrolled student to invite them into the iCan Dream Center community. The parent coach informs a social worker of the family's needs so the social worker can link each family to community resources if needed. One way a leader can assess the values of the organization is by analyzing the organization's budget and noting what that budget prioritizes. A leader can also look at reoccurring agenda topics as well as the actions the community chooses to celebrate.

Rituals and Ceremonies

Organizational rituals are routines with deeper significance (Deal & Peterson, 2016). These reoccurring activities have special meaning and historical context. Examples include welcoming students on the first day of school with applause, gifting new team members with school spirit wear, or setting time aside in meetings to acknowledge special accomplishments. Ceremonies are communal events which bind people together and often serve as an affirmation of unwritten values (Deal & Peterson, 2016). An example of a ceremony at iCan Dream Center is our annual Friendsgiving gathering where students are invited to bring a dish that represents a family tradition. This highly anticipated annual celebration affirms our commitment to honor diversity. Though it is not written as an explicit organizational value, it is embedded in the fabric of our organization.

Stories and Symbols

Telling and retelling stories "shape the patchwork of the culture" (Deal & Peterson, 2016, p. 82). Stories in an organization become meaningful symbols for the group. These symbols can represent problems, the standard for viable solutions, or outcomes to celebrate. Data discussions inundate and dominate schools, with educators' goal to improve student outcomes. While these important discussions have a place, educators may be missing opportunities to improve the experience of both learning and working by using stories to shape the culture that affects teachers' performance and students' experience.

What a Well School Culture Is *Not*

A well school culture is not a toxic culture. Toxic work cultures are unhappy places. Perhaps more than they can be seen, toxic cultures can be felt by all who enter, including students, parents, and guests. Working in a toxic culture makes what might be easy work difficult. Few feel safe enough to speak up in toxic cultures; fear is pervasive.

Deal and Peterson (2016) cite circumstances that unlock what constitutes a toxic culture through the school staff behaviors and beliefs. For example, in toxic cultures, staff view students as the problem, subcultures are critical of change, there is a lack of resource sharing, and suggestions for improvement are met with staff complaints. Gerald Ainomugisha (n.d.), a thought leader on corporate culture, posits the following list, which is not remotely exhaustive, of features of a toxic work environment.

- Low workplace morale
- An absence of effective communication
- Fear of supervisors
- Policies put ahead of people
- High staff turnover
- Cliques and groups are a source of tension
- A lack of delegated authority, so decision making is in the hands of few and often inaccessible employers

Can you identify any of the characteristics from Ainomugisha's (n.d.) list in your school? Notice a commonality among the characteristics—each creates a situation that magnifies and breeds negativity in people rather than drawing on and supporting their strengths. Toxic workplaces can become self-perpetuating.

Preventing, or in some cases healing, a toxic culture is *why* your leadership matters. You are the hero of your organization's story. The villains are the inevitable stress and chaos that can propagate within the walls of your school if left unchecked. When left on its own, stress turns toxic and sickens you, your educators, staff, and students. The cure is intentional, authentic leadership dedicated to ensuring those around you have the support they need to thrive. It's about designing an environment that treats employees like valued family members, where leaders support and empower teachers. The atmosphere becomes a part of the culture and defines the way of life inside your school. Creating cultures of wellness makes a significant impact in schools and doing so may be the highest form of achieving your purpose as an educational leader; it ensures the success of your students and teachers.

What a Well School Culture Is

In a well school culture, there is not just one educator who is the shining star—that one teacher perhaps who an outside visitor can immediately pick out as resilient, creative, thoughtful, and always respectful of others—the one students and staff alike love to be around. There isn't this one person in a well school culture because well school cultures offer an environment that is based in kindness and respect for all; that is, the culture is inherently supportive, thus allowing all teachers (and by extension all students) opportunities to be creative and develop the skills of resilience. You want your staff to be full of educators who are resilient, healthy in mind and body, and well-supported through the everyday trials of the educational system. Leaders can begin a healthy school culture by purposefully engineering an authentically supportive, nourishing, and compassionate environment.

The following sections offer ways to engineer this type of compassionate environment by introducing the trauma-compassionate approach and the people-first leadership philosophy. These actions and mindset together make up a framework for a culture of wellness that informs this book's content and the behaviors that guide leaders in their own learning communities. I'll further explore the trauma-compassionate approach, the people-first leadership philosophy, and the framework for a culture of wellness in chapters 3 (page 41) and 4 (page 57).

A Trauma-Compassionate Approach

A *trauma-compassionate approach* is one that honors the tenets of trauma-informed care. The purpose is to provide care and services to staff with compassion and empathy to prevent traumatizing or re-traumatizing staff members. In the trauma-compassionate approach, being *compassionate* is prized above simply being *informed* because the approach is grounded in a willingness to act on known information about how best to care for your team.

A People-First Leadership Philosophy

A *people-first leadership philosophy* honors the values, purpose, and humanity of team members, even beyond what they can contribute as employees of the organization. This philosophy holds at its core a willingness to serve your team while supporting the organizational vision. People-first leadership implements a positive, actionable belief system for creating the environment educators need to protect them from burnout and obtain favorable student outcomes.

The Framework for a Culture of Wellness

The framework for a culture of wellness supports a thriving environment that regards the welfare of each team member. People-first leadership is when team members feel their managers connect with, hear, value, trust, and support them. Additionally, leaders model trauma-compassionate strategies that become the standards for interactions within the organization. The result is a clear path that benefits educators, students, families, and the community. See figure 1.1 for a visual representation of how a trauma-compassionate approach and people-first leadership form the framework for a culture of wellness.

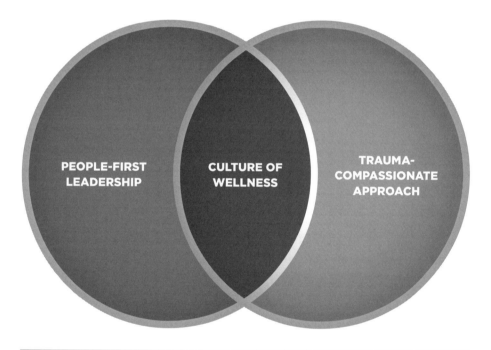

Figure 1.1: The framework for a culture of wellness.

The next chapter examines various forms of trauma, origins of trauma, and triggers in the workplace, and it unpacks the circumstances and consequences of environments with toxic stress.

Please use The Culture Within section to further explore the contents of this chapter through the lens of your own experiences, values, and perceptions.

The Culture Within

Recall an organization you worked for or spent time in prior to becoming a school or district leader. What did it feel like to be in that organization, physically, socially, emotionally? How did your interactions with other members of that organization feel? What do you think contributed to your experience of that organization's climate, and how, now that you are a leader yourself, can you use memories of that experience to influence what you bring to the climate in the organization you currently lead?

Refer to the discussion of Peterson's (2002) norms, values and beliefs, rituals and ceremonies, and symbols and stories from page 11. List one norm, one value or belief, one ritual or ceremony, and one symbol or story from your organization. What does each item on your list bring to the culture of your organization?

What is one change you could implement today to improve the work experience of your staff members?

CHAPTER 2

Pain Points

Trauma is a fact of life. It does not, however, have to be a life sentence.

—Peter A. Levine

One of my beloved team members at the iCan Dream Center, a high school teacher named Xiomara, sat in my office sobbing. I was focusing on being an empathetic presence and creating a safe space while also listening to the details, which seemed to be getting lost in her tears. Xiomara had come to my office completely disoriented and barely verbal. Her expression in those initial moments told me she was present only in the physical sense; emotionally, she was consumed with how she felt. Xiomara was one of my most veteran team members. I felt like I watched her grow up during her three-year tenure. She had begun to trust her own perspectives and contribute more substantively to group discussions. As her confidence increased, she was able to receive and apply corrective feedback without feeling personally assualted. As a result, she developed into an exceptional instructor. However, the reality is, Xiomara joined our team as an adult with experiences that would shape her interpretation of the event that led her to my office.

Xiomara had grown up in a household where rigid gender roles birthed toxic masculinity. Her father's physical abuse (predominantly directed toward her mother) was embedded in Xiomara's earliest memories. Unfortunately, those experiences remained very present for Xiomara because, as an adult educator, she still lived in her family home. The event that brought her to my office was this: Xiomara and a male colleague had a spirited debate during a team meeting. Later, at the end of the school day, the male colleague had approached Xiomara, positioning himself in the doorway of the office, in an attempt to resolve the matter. In that moment, Xiomara was triggered by what she perceived as a threat. She heard and saw her father—not a peer attempting to engage in a collegial dialogue. She fled to my office because, in that instant, she felt unsafe.

Xiomara and I processed the moment. I gave her my full attention as she shared what had occurred. With her permission, I placed my hand on her shoulder while speaking to her in a soft and calm tone. Eventually, she recognized there was no actual threat. Fortunately, the colleague who had triggered Xiomara's reaction was a social worker, and he extended a great deal of grace to restore equilibrium.

Xiomara's experience is a reminder for everyone: people do not check their trauma when they arrive at work. Traumas are travel companions present throughout their days. Trauma is a fact of life and can be experienced any place, any time, by anyone. A worldwide epidemiological general population study in twenty-four countries, with a combined sample of nearly seventy thousand adults across six continents, finds over 70 percent of respondents experienced at least one traumatic event in their lifetime, and 30.5 percent reported exposure to four or more traumatic events (Benjet et al., 2016). Further, five of the twenty-six categories included in the study accounted for over 50 percent of all exposures. Those five categories are as follows.

1. Witnessing death or serious injury
2. Experiencing the unexpected death of a loved one
3. Being mugged
4. Being in a life-threatening automobile accident
5. Experiencing a life-threatening illness or injury (Benjet et al., 2016)

Unpacking the evolution of the definition and study of trauma is essential to understanding how toxic stress becomes a form of trauma, and how toxic stress finds its way into the work environment. This chapter focuses on trauma and its impact on the workplace. I explore how the understanding of trauma has evolved and expanded, and look at the ways toxic environments can exacerbate the impact of trauma and undermine teacher performance. This chapter explores some of the triggers or *pain points* educators experience. The pages ahead illuminate the need for informed leaders who understand the compound impact of stressors and how they may contribute to burnout. They also lay the foundations for trauma-compassionate strategies, a critical component in the formation of a culture of wellness. Consider using the reproducible tool, "Leadership ACEs Survey" (page 38), featured at the end of the chapter both pre- and post-reading, to get a sense of your changing understanding of childhood trauma and its potential impact on educators' performance.

Foundational Knowledge About Trauma

Trauma (n.d.) is generally defined as "a physical injury (such as a wound)" or "a mental condition caused by severe shock, stress or fear, especially when the harmful effects last for a long time." The definition of *physical trauma* is straightforward; the definition of *psychological trauma* is a little more ambiguous. Understanding of psychological trauma has a complex history; taking a close look at the evolution of post-traumatic stress disorder (PTSD) as a diagnosis can help clarify.

When the American Psychiatric Association (APA; 1987) first included PTSD in the *Diagnostic and Statistical Manual of Mental Disorders*, the leading criteria for the condition was "a history of exposure to severe stress." In a history and overview of PTSD, Matthew J. Friedman (n.d.), a psychiatry professor and founding director of the National Center for PTSD, notes the manual's original conceptualization of *a traumatic event*:

> A catastrophic stressor that was outside the range of usual human experience . . . such as war, torture, rape, the Nazi Holocaust, the atomic bombings of Hiroshima and Nagasaki, natural disasters (such as earthquakes, hurricanes, and volcano eruptions), and human-made disasters (such as factory explosions, airplane crashes, and automobile accidents).

In the years following the APA's first designation of a traumatic event, studies reveal psychological trauma also appears after more commonplace stressful events and after a much broader range of types of traumatic experiences, including child abuse, sexual abuse, unexpected death of loved ones, life-threatening accidents, and (as Xiomara identified in her story at the beginning of this chapter) domestic violence (Drexler, Quist-Nelson, & Weil, 2022; Felitti et al., 1998; Georgsdottir, Sigurdardottir, & Gunnthorsdottir, 2021). The most notable research, conducted between 1995 and 1997, shedding light on the relationship between traumatic events and PTSD-like symptoms, is the well-known adverse childhood experiences study (Felitti et al., 1998). This study reveals a relationship between psychological trauma and what the study identifies as *adverse childhood experiences* (*ACEs*). In the study, a questionnaire about ACEs was mailed to nearly fourteen thousand adults who had completed a standardized medical evaluation. More than 70 percent responded. Those who suffered from one or more ACEs had physical changes in brain development, their body's reaction to stress, the development of chronic health issues, emotional and cognitive impairment, and the adoption of health-risk behaviors like smoking and overeating (Centers for Disease Control and Prevention [CDC], 2019). Some of the potential ACEs the study identifies include growing up in a home with violence, abuse, or neglect; suicide attempts or death by suicide of a loved one; and substance abuse and mental health issues (CDC, 2022). Survivors of these traumatic events can potentially suffer from symptoms similar to those diagnosed with PTSD (New Perspectives, n.d.).

Psychological trauma can result from a wide array of potentially traumatic events people may experience, from war and other catastrophic experiences to everyday happenings inside a home, including stressors people consider painful but not catastrophic (for example, "divorce, failure, rejection, serious illness, financial reverses, and the like" [Friedman, n.d.]).

The bottom line is that everyday occurrences have the potential to cause emotional trauma and stress. The key to managing the stress and chaos of life ties to how long the trauma endures, how often people are subjected to the events, the availability of support, and the coping skills people possess. As a school leader, it is imperative that you understand the consequences of stress. The supports accessible through the school, department, or organization will reduce the negative effects of stress, giving your team members a chance to succeed.

Classifying trauma into three subtypes—(1) acute, (2) chronic, and (3) complex—facilitates the understanding of the effects of the event on an individual. The differences between these three types of trauma are primarily based on the duration and persistence of the trauma, and the symptoms that may present in an individual.

1. *Acute trauma* refers to a single, isolated distressing event that threatens a person's physical safety and emotional security. Events such as a physical assault or rape, an accident or a natural disaster, or severe physical trauma may trigger acute trauma (Bence, 2021). Symptoms might present as elevated anxiety or panic, irritation, lack of trust, inability to focus, aggressive behavior, a lack of self-care, or the inability to sleep (Allarakha, 2021).

2. *Chronic trauma* is the repeated and sustained exposure to traumatic events and experiences over time (Allarakha, 2021), and the events generally involve an interpersonal relationship (Bence, 2021). Events that may cause chronic trauma include combat, domestic abuse, long-term illnesses, sexual abuse, domestic violence, and bullying. Individuals may present with emotional symptoms including extreme anger, flashbacks, unpredictable emotional outbursts, anxiety, and trust issues as well as physical symptoms such as head and body aches, fatigue, and nausea (Allarakha, 2021).

3. *Complex trauma* is what the National Child Traumatic Stress Network (n.d.) defines as a combination of both acute and chronic trauma. These

traumas "usually occur early in life and can disrupt many aspects of the child's development and the formation of a sense of self" (NCTSN, n.d.). Complex trauma results from exposure to a range of traumatic events which are "generally within the context of an interpersonal relationship . . . and may give the person a feeling of being trapped . . . and has a severe impact on the person's mind" (Allarakha, 2021). Domestic abuse, witnessing abuse in the home, neglect, starvation, and homelessness are also examples of chronically traumatic situations (Bence, 2021). Because the body's stress responses stay elevated rather than return to a baseline cognitive state, chronic trauma potentially affects the person's overall health, relationships, and performance at work or school (Allarakha, 2021).

The prevalence of psychological trauma in the United States is high. To provide perspective, according to the National Center for PTSD (2021), an estimated 6 percent of the U.S. adult population is diagnosed with PTSD at some point in its lifetime. Additionally, approximately 61 percent of adults suffer at least one ACE, while one in six adults experience four or more types of ACEs (CDC, 2019). Based on these statistics, leaders can safely assume that the adults they serve are bringing some ACEs to work daily. So why do some people exhibit continued effects of trauma while others recover from traumatic experiences?

Responses to Traumatic Stressors

Simply put, humans don't respond to traumatic stressors in a homogeneous way. Two people can experience the same traumatic event at the same time, and one possesses the ability to recover while the other may experience the trauma for a lifetime. Everyone is different. Friedman (n.d.) notes:

> Trauma, like pain, is not an external phenomenon that can be completely objectified. Like pain, the traumatic experience is filtered through cognitive and emotional processes before it can be appraised as an extreme threat. Because of individual differences in this appraisal process, different people appear to have different trauma thresholds, some more protected from and some more vulnerable to developing clinical symptoms after exposure to extremely stressful situations.

This explains why some people respond with fight, some flight, some hide, some freeze, and some appease (or fawn) during a traumatic event and its aftermath (Hammond, 2015). Mia Belle Frothingham (2021), a Harvard undergraduate student studying biology and psychology, explains the terms:

- **Fight:** facing any perceived threat aggressively
- **Flight:** running away from the danger

- **Freeze:** unable to move or act against a threat
- **Fawn [appease]:** immediately acting to try to please to avoid any conflict

The *limbic system* in the brain essentially shunts all unimportant-at-the-time systems in the body to focus on the systems that will save your life. Think of the bear that wanders into your campground. The "emergency lights" in your head flip to the *on* position; your body responds automatically by increasing your heart rate, dilating your blood vessels, lungs, and pupils, and produces the stress hormone cortisol so your body can do what it needs to do to respond to the threat (Frothingham, 2021). Your body also prepares a psychological response: your attention might intensify and your situational assessment speeds up. People see responses like this in the wilderness all the time; the animal kingdom is great at it. When the threat goes away, the *parasympathetic nervous system* takes over again, the emergency lights go dark, and the body returns to its normal cognitive state. People move on, albeit a bit frazzled. And they hopefully have a great story.

However, people who live with chronic or complex trauma don't return to a natural cognitive state when the threat retreats; the emergency lights never turn *off* (Frothingham, 2021). The brain remains on constant alert to cope with feelings of insecurity, fear, despair, traumatic memories, and the other symptoms of psychological trauma. These people are always in *survival mode* (Lebow, 2021). The longer the body functions in survival mode, the more likely the body and brain recognize this state as a new normal. In survival mode, the body and mind maintain the symptoms of complex trauma: flashbacks, lapses in memory, difficulty regulating emotions, being on alert, depersonalization, sleep disturbances and nightmares, difficult interpersonal relationships, low self-esteem, and avoidance of people, places, and scenarios that upset (Lebow, 2021). As people who suffer from chronic or complex trauma move through life always on alert (emergency lights always flashing with little or no support), they begin to live every day with a heightened sense of vulnerability, fear, and stress. Leaders can use this understanding of the effects of trauma to recognize behaviors in educators as not irrational or arbitrary, but maybe responses to traumatic experiences. More critically, leaders can begin to conceptualize these responses as, while not ideal, valid, important, and even in a sense, reasonable. It is paramount that leaders remain aware of reactions. Some responses, even seemingly benign ones (like appeasement), should elicit support from leaders in a culture of wellness.

Vicarious Trauma and Its Connection to Teachers

Another form of trauma particularly relevant to educators is *vicarious trauma* because of how it affects those in what some call the *helper professions*. Some often use the term *vicarious trauma* as a synonym for *secondary traumatic stress*; the definition is the experience of trauma symptoms resulting from exposure to other people's trauma and their stories of traumatic events (GoodTherapy.org Team, 2016). *Secondary traumatic stress* is similarly explained as the emotional duress that results when an individual hears about the firsthand trauma experiences of another.

Vicarious trauma is a significant source of stress in the teaching environment as well as in other caregiver professions like social services, medicine, law enforcement, emergency medical services, and victim services because these people often work with victims of trauma (Walker, 2019). Teachers see trauma every day in school.

Your students experience all types of trauma, including extreme trauma such as the grief from the death of a parent or sibling, a severe accident, child abuse, or sexual abuse. But as I've discussed, trauma also results from seemingly less-traumatic circumstances like poverty and neglect. But these are still traumatic circumstances. A student may experience food insecurity, homelessness, or feel unseen by caregivers. These are basic needs, and when they're unmet, it is traumatic.

Effective teachers make connections with their students, which provide insight into each student's emotional distress. The compounded effect of experiencing trauma vicariously through students and an inability to cope with daily stress results in burnout for educators. Recovery can prove difficult, particularly in toxic environments.

Here are some actions leaders can take to support their teachers and staff to help prevent burnout from daily stresses and the stress of vicarious trauma.

- **Reflect:** One of the most critical steps you can take to set a supportive tone for your team is self-awareness. You will need to take a quick inventory of your own state of mind when someone is in crisis to ensure you can offer meaningful support. If you are in a state of burnout yourself, it is unlikely that you can lend regulation to your team members. Use the reproducible "Burnout Risk Scale" (page 36) to proactively determine your own burnout risk and take the necessary steps for personal wellness.

- **Be present:** Being present is critical during times of crisis. Leaders must use self-control to close their laptops, put away their cellphones, and bring their minds to the present moment. A steady presence, particularly during times of emotional dysregulation, is therapeutic. I'll spend some time unpacking this later in the book as a vital component in trauma-compassionate leadership.

- **Model:** Speak to your team members using a calm, low tone. You will have to regulate yourself so you do not unintentionally escalate situations by being reactive. Breathe slowly and deeply. Consider leading the team in a deep-breaching exercise.
- **Listen:** I cannot emphasize this enough! As a leader, you must express a positive curiosity while suspending judgment, giving advice, and developing quick solutions. In your leadership role, you are responsible for problem solving but the reality is that when a person is in crisis, that person may not be prepared for solutions. Generally, the person in crisis simply needs a space to emote.

Toxic Stress as a Form of Trauma

Like trauma, stress is also a fact of life. *Positive stress*, also called *acute stress*, is normal and good for people. It even has a name: *eustress* (n.d.). It's the response people's bodies have to nonthreatening, challenging experiences that excite and motivate them. People experience positive stress when they get a new job, start a new business, get married, or try a new sport for the first time, and it has positive effects on the body (Lamoreux, 2021). Experiencing positive stress (such as that from a job promotion, preparing for a wedding, or purchasing a new home) results in a mild release of stress hormones that move people to action (Jamieson, 2019). Eustress is beneficial and allows people to live outside their comfort zone. But it's the negative stress that makes the headlines and keeps people awake at night.

Negative stress falls into two main categories: (1) tolerable and (2) toxic. People experience *tolerable stress*, also known as *distress* with normal, everyday events (that is, these events happen to someone every day, not that someone experiences these events every day) associated with negative outcomes. The death of a loved one, divorce, punishment, or an injury are examples of instances where tolerable stress is present; there's a beginning and an end to the experience (Lamoreux, 2021).

The term *toxic stress* is relatively new. Because it is about the impact of long-term stress, it is typically defined in terms of children's experiences. In contrast to positive and tolerable stress, *toxic stress* is defined as:

> Strong, frequent, and/or prolonged adversity—such as physical or emotional abuse, chronic neglect, caregiver substance abuse or mental illness, exposure to violence, and/or the accumulated burdens of family economic hardship—without adequate adult support. This kind of prolonged activation of the stress response systems can disrupt the development of brain architecture and other organ systems and increase the risk for stress-related disease and cognitive impairment, well into the adult years. (Center on the Developing Child, 2015)

So how is toxic stress a form of trauma for educators in the workplace? The following sections explore how stress enters the workplace through staff members and then develops into a form of continuing trauma, and how the stressful nature of the work itself can propagate toxic stress that leads to trauma.

How Toxic Stress Finds Its Way Into the Workplace

Based on the number of adults ACEs affect and those who've suffered trauma in their lifetime, people see traumatized adults in the workplace every day. Educators bring their trauma to work and feel vulnerable and insecure, which affects how and what they do, and their relationships with colleagues and students.

People also experience toxic stress that originates in the workplace. Exposure to these toxic environments creates trauma and stress in people's lives, and they bring that trauma home. Walking into a toxic work environment would feel the same as walking into your home every day after school when you are an abused and neglected child, and vice versa. Leaders don't want teachers walking into schools like they may have walked into homes where they experienced abuse and fear, and not knowing if they'll be celebrated or berated. Work can be a safe place.

As an educational leader, it is up to you to interrupt those cycles, so your teachers feel vulnerable in a way that results in them being innovative and creative on behalf of the students, but not vulnerable in a way that leaves them fearful and afraid. The goal is for educators to take risks trying new interventions or developing new approaches to serve students. A toxic environment hinders progress. For example, fear of retribution may immobilize a teacher from sharing that she is unsure of how to implement an instructional practice.

Sources of Toxic Stress at Work

Stress in the workplace is normal, and no profession is immune. While educational leaders cannot influence environments outside their schools, they can and are obliged to influence and create environments within their schools where they celebrate teachers, and teachers feel safe.

Sources of toxic stress present (and perhaps abundant) in some educational organizations include the following.

- Racism (unequal enforcement of policies, microaggressions)
- Poor work boundaries (demand for long work hours, frequent or habitual supervisor contact outside work hours)
- Job insecurity (unclear performance expectations, nepotism)
- Abusive supervisors (relational aggression, public criticism)

- Sexual harassment (unwanted compliments, unwelcome touching, sexually based quid pro quo)

Leaders must ensure they are not perpetuating any of these systemic stressors. Moreover, leaders should use their influence to alleviate the impact of these stressors when they do occur; leverage your position to advocate for your team members and commit to dismantling these systems and harmful practices. Additionally, it is your responsibility to ensure the conditions do not exist for toxicity to thrive.

The Burnout and Compassion Fatigue That Result From Toxic Stress

Teachers experience stress every day but might not take the time to reduce the stress in their lives. The consequences of perpetually stressed-out teachers in classrooms include low performance, poor health, increased absenteeism, and high teacher-turnover rates. Teachers take the stress home, and the consequences take effect there too. Most importantly, it also affects the educational outcomes of students, leading to "lower student achievement, lower continuity for students and parents, and higher education costs" (Pennsylvania State University, 2016, p. 4).

Once stress levels reach the point where they affect the health, motivation, performance, relationships, and almost everything else in life, teachers arrive at burnout. *Merriam-Webster* says *burnout* (n.d.) is "exhaustion of physical or emotional strength or motivation usually as a result of prolonged stress or frustration." The transitive verb definition also applies, "to cause to fail, wear out, or become exhausted especially from overwork or overuse" (Burnout, n.d.).

I dug a little deeper. According to the World Health Organization (WHO, 2019), *burnout* is not a medical condition but an "occupational phenomenon, . . . a syndrome conceptualized as resulting from chronic workplace stress that has not been successfully managed." The WHO (2019) defines three dimensions of burnout:

- feelings of energy depletion or exhaustion
- increased mental distance from one's job, or feelings of negativism or cynicism related to one's job
- reduced professional efficacy

Once educators enter a state of burnout, it can become toxic to everyone. I have personally witnessed teacher burnout: the teachers' classroom performance falters; they miss more work; they quit (often with little or no notice); their relationships with students, colleagues, and family members deteriorate; and there is a considerable shift in their perspective on life. They lose joy, commitment, and, most importantly, compassion (Walker, 2019).

Compassion for others is probably the single most important characteristic teachers possess. A desire to act on this compassion may even be the primary reason many enter the field of education. However, the "heart" teachers approach their jobs with has an inherent cost: *compassion fatigue*. Compassion fatigue kicks in when you stop feeling compassion and empathy for your students, colleagues, and perhaps even your family and friends. How does this occur? *Compassion fatigue* refers to the intense physical, mental, and emotional erosion that occurs when teachers provide care to another and cannot refuel (Walker, 2019). These teachers have nothing left to give. Ultimately, teachers can become devoid of any compassion they once possessed.

The result of compassion fatigue is an erosion in educators' ability to make effective decisions that affect their colleagues and students. Admittedly, when I go to work, I don't think intellectually about what is required of me to do my work. I just do it. But if you take a moment to look at what is mentally and physiologically required of you to make decisions, complete tasks, meet challenges, and connect with people every day (in short, *function*), the effect of stress on your mind and body becomes clearer. The same is true of the teachers you work with and support, which makes it paramount that you recognize signs of burnout and compassion fatigue.

Impaired Executive Functioning as a Consequence of Toxic Stress

Executive functioning—your higher cognitive functions—describes an array of skills one uses all day, every day, at home, at play, and at work. Skills associated with executive functioning include planning and organizing, concentrating and controlling mental focus, analyzing and processing information, and controlling emotions and behavior (Villines, 2019). How well do you execute these functions when you are operating at optimum? When acutely stressed? When chronically stressed?

Poor executive functioning is associated with several medical diagnoses, including attention deficit hyperactivity disorder (ADHD), bipolar disorder, schizophrenia, and autism (Villines, 2019). Not surprisingly, poor executive functioning is also associated with stress (Tyler, 2020). Some of the symptoms of poor executive functioning include:

- trouble managing emotions or impulses
- problems with starting, organizing, planning, or completing tasks
- trouble listening or paying attention
- short-term memory issues
- inability to multitask or balance tasks

- socially inappropriate behavior
- inability to learn from past consequences
- difficulty solving problems
- difficulty learning or processing new information (Villines, 2019).

When teachers are stressed, it is the students who bear the long- and short-term consequences. I have observed teachers who are unable to plan and organize in a way that maximizes their ability to facilitate instruction. When teachers are stressed, they can't take those sequential steps, have poor self-regulation, are more apt to yell at a student, and are emotionally unavailable, maybe even sitting on a bench in a bathroom. In their heightened state of stress, teachers tend to communicate poorly (and in a problematic manner) with students and colleagues because their proper response to a stimulus is impaired.

Perhaps the most crucial element of executive functioning for teachers is *impulse control*. When a person is chronically stressed, there's no gap between a triggering input and the nearly automated, probably inappropriate response. Under these conditions, teachers lose the ability to take the time their brain needs to sort out the trigger and a proper response. That's why seemingly small transgressions might evoke responses like raising voices, yelling at a student, or making a sarcastic remark when a nurturing approach is what's needed when relating to students and colleagues. Stress causes teachers to respond in a way that's not tempered or thoughtful; these interactions can have lasting effects for those on the receiving end—students and colleagues—and can last a long, long time. This compounds the toxic-stress recipe in districts and schools with already dysfunctional cultures because this is how teachers show up when working in an environment that's not nurturing.

Given that a nurturing environment is the one thing educational leaders have the power, responsibility, privilege, and honor to mitigate for teachers, it falls on leaders to establish a schoolwide culture of wellness where the various forms of trauma and toxic stress everyone experiences in some form meet with compassion. Poor work boundaries, job insecurity, poor relationships, abusive supervisors, sexual harassment—these are all issues in a school environment educational leaders can set a standard for and mitigate. The purpose of this book is to guide you, a courageous and compassionate leader, to develop a culture of wellness. While this chapter provides reasons *why* this culture is necessary, the chapter ahead articulates *how* to meet stress and trauma with compassion.

Please use The Culture Within section to further explore the contents of this chapter through the lens of your own experiences, values, and perceptions.

The Culture Within

How does becoming aware of your own feelings of burnout affect how you view the challenges your teachers and staff members face and their feelings that stem from these challenges?

What new insights do you have on the impact of stress on functioning? How has your perspective on the needs of struggling teachers shifted after reading this chapter?

How does understanding toxic stress as trauma motivate you to action as a leader? When you examine your own best approaches, do you find any of your practices unintentionally contribute to the stress of your teachers and staff members? If so, in what ways can you adjust your approaches to be more supportive?

_____
_____
_____
_____
_____
_____
_____
_____
_____
_____
_____
_____
_____
_____
_____
_____
_____
_____
_____
_____
_____
_____
_____
_____
_____
_____
_____

Burnout Risk Scale

Burnout emerges over time and patterns of unhealthy coping can trigger it. The results of this assessment will help to determine your risk for burnout.

Rate yourself on each of the items in the following table and signify how the indicators apply to your work habits.

	Rarely (1)	Sometimes (2)	Frequently (3)	Almost Always (4)
Working long hours				
Having trouble delegating				
Working without breaks				
Acquiescing when you'd rather say no				
Bottling up feelings rather than expressing them				
Procrastinating or avoiding tasks				
Showing up as a perfectionist				
Taking work home				
Putting aside hobbies due to workload				
Taking on unenjoyable issues or projects outside your job duties				
TOTAL SCORES				
GRAND TOTAL:				

Once you calculate your grand total, use the following table to determine your current burnout risk.

1–10	11–20	21–30	31–40
No risk for burnout Continue your positive coping strategies (for example, make a daily gratitude list).	**Low risk for burnout** Set time aside for self-reflection on your response to stress (for example, evaluate what went well during your workday).	**Moderate risk for burnout** Note the areas where you scored a 3 or 4 and make a plan to implement some positive coping strategies (for example, build in time for hobbies and enjoyable activities).	**High risk for burnout** Take immediate action (for example, contact a psychotherapist; seek support to improve your emotional wellness and ensure effectiveness in your personal and professional lives).

Reflect and brainstorm next steps.

Leadership ACEs Survey

Use this tool to measure your beliefs about the impact of adverse childhood experiences (ACEs) on your own leadership and on your teachers. Take the survey both before and after reading chapter 2 (page 21) and reflect on how your thoughts about the impact of adverse childhood experiences on educators change.

Rate each of the following statements on a scale of 1–5.

Scale:

1—Strongly disagree
2—Somewhat disagree
3—Somewhat agree
4—Agree
5—Strongly agree

I believe ACEs have an impact on teacher performance.

1	2	3	4	5

I believe my approach as a leader can make a difference in my team's success.

1	2	3	4	5

I believe my own ACEs score affects how I react to my teachers' behavior.

1	2	3	4	5

I believe my own resilience has affected my life in a positive way.

1	2	3	4	5

I believe work environments have an impact on school personnel affected by ACEs.

1	2	3	4	5

I have a solid understanding of toxic stress as a form of trauma.

1	2	3	4	5

I learned new concepts for understanding the ways toxic stress finds its way into the work environment.

1	2	3	4	5

I feel the brain research on trauma is a motivator for me to make necessary changes in my approach with my team.

1	2	3	4	5

I believe the more our school can create a safe space for our teachers, the greater chance they have to successfully support students.

1	2	3	4	5

Reflect:

CHAPTER 3

Trauma-Informed Compassion

> Someone who has experienced trauma also has gifts to offer all of us—in their depth, their knowledge of our universal vulnerability, and their experience of the power of compassion.
>
> —Sharon Salzberg

I arrived at work on what felt like a typical Friday morning in the final stretch of the school year. It had been a tense week for the students I served as a social worker in my first school-based role after graduate school—a high school on the South Side of Chicago. My focus was on getting through the day and joining friends to commence the weekend. School would not begin for over an hour, but my students (most of whom were homeless) would often gather in my office for food, bus passes, a listening ear, and everything in between.

As I approached the building, I saw a throng of residents, police officers, and the media starting to gather. The scene was not out of the ordinary for our school, so based on previous experiences I knew I had a short window of time before the crowd got too thick to pass through. I quickly gathered my belongings, exited my car, and flashed my staff ID as I pressed through the crowd. What I did not anticipate—could not have anticipated—was seeing my student, Marcus, lying lifeless and bloody at the school entrance. Several weeks earlier, my director had reprimanded me for taking Marcus in my personal vehicle to the county hospital to obtain medication. To say that Marcus and his twin brother were my most beloved students is an understatement.

I was on autopilot as I entered the building and tended to the emotional needs of the students and staff. About midway through the day, I was called to the central office. I was relieved to leave the building for a private moment to process all that had occurred. I cried for what felt like hours but was actually only for the twenty-minute car ride from the southside to downtown Chicago. To my surprise, upon my arrival, I was reprimanded for not contacting the correct supervisor. I had made a quick phone call to the program supervisor, whom I interacted with most frequently, rather than my director. That director accused me of not having followed protocol because I was angry with her.

In truth, I hadn't followed the protocol because I was not trained in the crisis procedure. In addition, despite my director being both a fellow human being and a licensed psychotherapist, it never occurred her that Marcus's death had caused me to experience my own trauma. In that moment, my director was not concerned with my feelings or how to best offer support, and although I received an apology the following week, irreparable damage was done. This was the first time I truly pondered the demands of effective leadership.

This chapter examines *trauma-informed care*—what it is and why it is an important part of effective leadership—and how trauma-compassionate leadership approaches extend and deepen the reach of trauma-informed care by promoting a kind, supportive learning environment that functions like a healthy, caring family.

Trauma-Informed Care and Its Contribution to Effective Leadership

If *trauma* "is the response to a deeply distressing or disturbing event that overwhelms an individual's ability to cope, causes feelings of helplessness, diminishes their sense of self and their ability to feel a full range of emotions and experiences" (Unyte Integrated Listening Systems, 2018), then a trauma-informed approach for leaders assumes that there will be individuals with a history of trauma and recognition of the role that trauma plays in individuals' lives (University at Buffalo, n.d.). The purpose of a *trauma-informed approach* is to provide care and services with compassion and empathy in an effort to prevent re-traumatization of the people in your charge.

Beginning in the 1970s, the healthcare industry increasingly included the practice of trauma-informed care when deliberating diagnosis and treatment for trauma victims. This approach assumes an individual is likely to have a history of trauma (Substance Abuse and Mental Health Services Administration, 2014). The approach was part of an effort among those in the medical field to study behavioral symptoms Vietnam veterans experienced, sometimes years after these veterans had experienced the trauma (Curi, 2018).

The understanding gained from those early studies of trauma in Vietnam veterans launched a series of studies in the decades following involving victims of trauma, including children and their families. The formal conclusion was that because ACEs can be widespread and have a lifelong impact for some, leaders should apply trauma-informed care over a broad range of social services (Substance Abuse and Mental Health Services Administration, 2014). Trauma-informed care emerged in the fields of mental health, substance abuse, child welfare, criminal justice systems, and, yes, schools.

The following sections help leaders conceptualize the importance of trauma-informed care by describing the impact of an absence of trauma-informed care in education, the CDC's six guiding principles of trauma-informed care, and trauma-informed care in practice.

When Education Isn't Trauma Informed

Unless tragedy strikes, children—including those who experienced ACEs—will inevitably matriculate into adulthood. In the best-case scenario, these adults received the support they needed to cope with the effects of trauma, achieve their learning goals, and move forward in life beyond high school. While young people who don't receive such support may successfully figure out how to navigate their K–12 years on their own and move forward, many do not. For some, their lived trauma acts as a drag on their ability to achieve life goals, while the most unfortunate never find a solid footing in their lives. While it's understandable your thoughts at this point have turned to your students, also bear in mind that, inevitably, there are educators in your charge who fit this description.

Nadine Burke-Harris, California's first surgeon general, is a proponent of approaches to trauma-informed care that support students through their K–12 education. Burke-Harris does this by dedicating her career to changing the way society responds to childhood trauma (Gaines & Pratt-Kielley, 2019). Burke-Harris's lifelong dream, born from her experience as a pediatrician working in an underserved community, is to screen every student for childhood trauma and provide appropriate intervention (Gaines & Pratt-Kielley, 2019). As a pediatrician, Burke-Harris found a high number of children referred to her for ADHD did not meet the criteria for such a diagnosis. She instead found many of her patients had experienced severe trauma, which affected not just their behaviors but also their bodies (Gaines & Pratt-Kielley, 2019). Again, consider not just the implications of these findings on the students in your school or district but also on the teachers in your building who *were* students.

Trauma-informed care has reached a point of acceptance; social service organizations expect its application when treating patients who may be victims of ACEs (Substance Abuse and Mental Health Services Administration, 2014).

However, the majority of schools are not equipped to screen every student or staff member for ACEs or assess their coping skills to know what forms of trauma-informed care will be most effective. Nonetheless, thought leaders and legislators increasingly encourage educational systems to adopt trauma-informed practices school- and districtwide (Trauma-Informed Care for Children and Families Act, 2017).

Educators each have their "personal backpack of stuff to carry around," and then, as teachers, they also have to do the heavy lifting for students. It's no wonder compassion fatigue and burnout set in when there are less-than-ideal workplace environments. Thus, it's imperative for leaders to design environments that cultivate wellness and create opportunities for people to be their best. Employers and school leaders may not be empowered or trained to directly assess peoples' behaviors, health, or coping skills, but they *can* design environments that cultivate wellness to support those who feel broken and in need of healing spaces. Thus, understanding the core principles that can establish and sustain trauma-informed approaches benefits all.

CDC's Six Guiding Principles to Trauma-Informed Practices

The CDC (2020) has published guidelines in cooperation with the Substance Abuse and Mental Health Services Administration and the National Center for Trauma-Informed Care. U.S. organizations, including schools, first-response agencies, medical and nursing colleges, medical practices, and hospitals, have taken these guiding principles and adapted their approaches to trauma-informed care. Following are the CDC's (2020) six guiding principles to trauma-informed practices.

1. Safety is perhaps one of the most important principles of trauma-informed care. If people feel unsafe for any reason, trusting and transparent environments cannot exist. Leaders are obligated to ensure the work environment feels safe for all, including students, teachers, and support staff. Some practices organizations can implement to improve psychological and physical safety include:
   - Implementing trauma-informed supervision practices
   - Creating confidential or anonymous avenues for staff and clients to provide feedback
   - Reinforcing the importance of staff autonomy, choice, and empowerment
   - Training on organizational practices that promote safety and reduce the risk of workplace violence (Relias, n.d.)
2. Trustworthiness and transparency are key building blocks to a successful trauma-informed care program. The goal of *transparency* is to build *trust* (Trauma Informed Oregon, 2014). When teachers trust their leaders,

they feel safer. Students are the beneficiaries of transparent and trusting relationships.

3. Peer support (teachers supporting one another) and assisting one another in stress management are critical. Access to therapy, communication with supervisors and colleagues, paid time off, and trauma-informed care practices within the organization promote healing and reduce stress (Duquesne University School of Nursing, 2020).

4. In the same vein as *it takes a village* to provide a student a healthy learning environment, it also takes collaboration and mutuality from everyone in an organization to effectively support those experiencing trauma and the stress that accompanies it.

5. Empowerment is necessary, so voice and choice when supporting trauma survivors operates similarly to providing choices to young children. Providing a choice (like go to bed now or in ten minutes) seems to have an empowering effect when asking a child to do something they normally would not wish to do. Treating trauma survivors is similar; using a person's strengths provides the voice and choice when treating trauma (Duquesne University School of Nursing, 2020).

6. Recognition and respect for a person's cultural, historical, and gender perspectives are essential when instituting a successful trauma-informed care program. Consider cultural and historical experiences and gender-based experiences when responding to trauma to understand factors influencing individual responses (Health Care Toolbox, n.d.).

These guiding principles from the CDC (2020) provide direction to various organizations. The implementation will look different depending on the organization's population. For example, these applied principles are nuanced in different ways when a teacher implements them in a classroom versus when a department chair applies them for the benefit of a team.

Trauma-Informed Response in Practice

Trauma-informed care might look like this: imagine a student who is triggered when a teacher raises his, her, or their voice or uses a certain tone. When this occurs, the student might immediately react by swearing or kicking or striking out. If the teacher doesn't have knowledge of the student's background or the violence this student may have grown up with (which causes him, her, or them to react to certain tones and volume of voice triggers), the teacher could unknowingly exacerbate the situation. A trauma-informed approach would be to create a welcoming environment and speak positively and kindly to everyone—*no matter what*—mitigating triggered reactions from happening in the first place. The second part of the approach would be, if you do get that outburst, not to immediately condemn it. Instead, ask, "How can I help?"

From a leadership perspective, you must remember that adults are also survivors of trauma. Just because people reach adulthood doesn't mean they've found the magic elixir that heals. Adults have their pain points, and they overreact to triggers just as students do. And adults deserve compassion. So as a leader, what might this look like in terms of trauma-compassionate responses?

At one point during my time as an assistant superintendent, I was introducing a book study on trauma-informed practices to a room full of principals, which was ironic because at that time, I was an emotional wreck due to personal issues. After I explained the book study and what participation I expected, a woman piped up out of nowhere, "I'm not doing it."

Just as a teacher with a student refusing to engage in a lesson or assignment, this school principal put me in a position in which I was either going to flare up or pause and respond, rather than react. Because I was struggling emotionally at that time, I was basically in tears and saying to myself, "Are you kidding? Are you serious about this?" However, what I eventually said was, "Please hang back after the meeting." She did stay in the meeting without any subsequent outburst, and with that time to reflect, she did apologize.

What I found out after the incident was that this principal was struggling because she came to our district from a district where she had been an assistant superintendent. Due to the political climate in that district, she left the district and her previous role. Her new position as principal was essentially, to her, a demotion. Based on feedback from those with whom she worked most closely, her colleagues in our district did not receive her well. She was grappling with a lot—just like many others might in a similar situation. That was a struggle for her, and so being told to do something by someone in the role she just vacated (not to mention that I was twenty years younger than she was) was triggering. Refusal to comply was her pushback. While I may not have realized the reason behind her reaction at the time, when I put the pieces together later, I was grateful I didn't respond with a knee-jerk reaction.

This is one example of many typical for leaders. I previously discussed the fight, flight, freeze, or appease response when someone is triggered. The following content will help guide you connect trauma-informed leadership to trauma-compassionate approaches for establishing a culture of wellness.

From Trauma Informed to Trauma Compassionate

It was my growing sense of the importance of compassion in responding to people professionally and personally that made me begin to explore the reach of trauma-informed care and whether that reach is significant enough to cultivate the well culture I believe leaders should foster. This sense was compounded when I first heard the term *trauma compassionate* from Sarah Bess Dworin, a culture and climate consultant who believes that authentic relationships are the foundation for all meaningful learning (personal communication, May 20, 2021). Sarah is passionate about supporting schools to build community, engage in productive collaboration, and resolve conflict constructively. I attended a training where she taught her method. I then invited Sarah to the iCan Dream Center to talk to my team about trauma, and, more specifically, about how to implement her approaches, which my staff have since incorporated at the center.

During her presentation, Sarah chose to use the term *trauma compassionate* instead of *trauma informed*. She highlighted the importance of being compassionate in the face of trauma, a concept I ruminated on for a while, thinking deeply about the meaning of the word *compassion* in comparison to *informed*. *Informed* means to express a level of awareness through having information. *Compassion*—made up of *com*, meaning *with*, and *pati*, meaning *to suffer* (in Ancient Greek)—literally means *to suffer with*. *Greater Good Magazine* (n.d.) notes, "Among emotion researchers, [compassion] is defined as the feeling that arises when you are confronted with another's suffering and feel motivated to relieve that suffering."

I don't believe leaders can be compassionate without taking action. When I talk about the concept of trauma-informed care, it's simple for leaders to merely inform themselves. It's much more difficult for leaders to show the compassion required to alleviate suffering. Taking the action inherent in a compassionate approach is critical to developing a culture of wellness in your school. This is why compassion is part of the framework for a culture of wellness I discussed in chapter 1 (page 9), which informs the purpose of this book. The following section examines the trauma-compassionate approach component of the framework and discusses the behaviors this component encompasses.

The Trauma-Compassionate Approach and the Framework for a Culture of Wellness

As you see in figure 3.1 (page 48) the behaviors the framework identifies as trauma-compassionate align with the CDC's (2020) six principles of practice for individuals impacted by trauma and are critical to the nature of the trauma-compassionate approach.

Figure 3.1: The trauma-compassionate approach and the framework for a culture of wellness.

No matter your own sphere of influence, as a leader and human, you can approach the people you support with a sense of compassion and an understanding that while you may be unaware of the specific nature of the trauma they may be experiencing (personally or vicariously, at home or at work), you are there to support them.

As a leader, modeling compassion and informed practices will have a ripple effect on the organization. Team members will begin to make allowances for one another, trust will develop, and everyone will begin to work well as a unit. This unit may begin to feel like a healthy family in a culture of wellness. The following section explores this notion of the ideal work unit as similar to a healthy, high-functioning family.

The Organization as Family

Do you think of the people you work with as a second family or does your attitude more closely align with the sentiment, *I could never think of these people as family*. I want to illuminate further what it means when I say "a family-oriented team," because I think often organizations have said, "Hey, we're a family," but use that rhetoric to manipulate people in exploitative ways (into working an extra hour, taking on that extra project, or grappling with issues they aren't equipped to resolve). This is much more dysfunctional than functional. And I think I'd be remiss not to make it clear when some readers hear *family-like* or *family-like environment*, they will have their own response that might connect to being burned out, misused, or exploited.

At the iCan Dream Center, I qualify our "we are a family" stance and say "we *connect* to one another." One of our organizational core values is connection. *Connection* to center staff means we relate to one another like a functional family. (I do acknowledge that no one family or organization is 100 percent functional or dysfunctional—there are always shades of gray.) In this context, it means we intentionally take the time to get to know one another. We get to a point where we understand one another's peculiarities, and we make allowances for them. And we still invite everyone to take a seat at the table. The goal in a culture of wellness is to institute practices that allow all team members to maintain a sense of belonging.

For me, connecting with one another at the center mirrors how staff connect within their own families, provided those conceptions of family are healthy and functional—that is, being aware of one another's needs and extending grace. When center staff encounter situations that have to do with someone who has, for example, a unique approach to the world that might chafe us a little bit, we are still inclusive. People all have relatives who drink a little too much, whose quirks or idiosyncrasies get on their nerves, who hold different political views that feel infuriating, and so on. Our staff encounter these same people in the workplace too. Like family, the center staff still accept them. And, as leaders, we still celebrate their contributions.

People know thriving and positive organizations by their shared celebrations and traditions. If you and your staff execute them effectively, celebratory practices and traditions "communicate and solidify values, celebrate core accomplishments, and build a close-fitting sense of community" (Deal and Peterson, 2016, p. 121). As a leader, you must seek opportunities to cultivate a sense of belonging. Traditions will be enjoyable, but you have an opportunity to increase social impact as well. For example, the average Canadian woman makes 87 cents for every dollar that a man earns (Statistics Canada, 2017). This disparity is not uncommon in nations around the world, which creates an opportunity to celebrate by raising awareness and celebrating the contributions of women. At the iCan Dream Center on International Women's Day, each team member purchases women's items (from nail polish to sanitary products), which they submit as admission to an after-hours party. The center staff later ship the items to organizations in developing countries committed to supporting vulnerable girls and women. See the reproducible "Traditions and Celebrations Planning Tool" (page 55) for more ideas for traditions to create, and events and shared experiences to celebrate.

In the workplace, just like in your own family, staff members enjoy one another, yet they must respect limits and boundaries to relationships. For example, workplace bullying and harassment are behaviors that reach across the boundaries of what is acceptable and respectful among colleagues. Often associated with childhood, bullying does indeed extend into adulthood for both those who are bullied and those doing the bullying. In the workplace, bullying behavior is often referred to as *relational aggression*, which constitutes behaviors such as personal insults, mean jokes, shaming, humiliation, exclusion, taking credit, and even making threats, to name a few of its forms (Stuck & Byars, 2022). It's equally important to acknowledge those who engage in unacceptable behavior are not inherently bad people; they are most likely in survival mode themselves. But again, they are adults, and it is incumbent on you, as a leader, to address the issues head on and put the onus on the adults to behave differently.

Anthony Dallmann-Jones, also known as Dr. DJ, is a psychotherapist who focuses on family dynamics. He cites a number of attributes of both functional and dysfunctional families (Dallmann-Jones, 2019). I use those attributes as inspiration for similar attributes that apply in the workplace (see table 3.1). Consider the behaviors that characterize your workplace, and how you, as the leader, can promote healthy, functional behaviors among colleagues.

Table 3.1: Functional Versus Dysfunctional Work Family Behaviors

Functional	Dysfunctional
Affirms one another	Disparages one another
Focuses on the well-being of team members	Hyper-focuses on productivity
Receives effective training	Demands performance outcomes without training or orientation
Considers social and physical wellness	Discounts health needs
Sees problems as opportunities for solution-oriented collaboration	Ignores problems
Treats mistakes as opportunities for growth	Spotlights mistakes or shames others for mistakes
Encourages autonomy and creativity	Expects quiet conformity
Cultivates psychological safety	Sees criticism and hypervigilance as ways of life

Source: Adapted from Dallmann-Jones, 2019.

In conclusion, trauma-compassionate organizational leadership looks like family in that the organizational leaders take the time, care, and diligence to foster what is best for those they lead, and they do it with compassion in a safe environment they've created—where people can be their best. When these leaders encounter those who stray beyond the bounds of what's acceptable, they recognize, call out, and correct the behavior.

Chapter 4 (page 57) articulates how to link the trauma-compassionate approach with the servant and transformational leadership approaches that together encompass a people-first leadership philosophy to nurture a flourishing culture of wellness. Trauma-compassionate leadership grounded in people-first leadership is the foundation of a culture of wellness.

Please use The Culture Within section to further explore the contents of this chapter through the lens of your own experiences, values, and perceptions.

The Culture Within

How do your relationships with your colleagues reflect the functional or dysfunctional workplace behaviors in table 3.1 (page 50)?

How would your organization be different if you instituted trauma-compassionate leadership?

What would an authentic family-like workspace look like to you? How would the workspace staff behave and interact with one another on a daily basis? In what ways would they offer support to one another? How would they confront the challenges of conflict?

___

Traditions and Celebrations Planning Tool

Creating shared traditions and opportunities to celebrate is critical in connecting and creating a sense of belonging among a team. Your team likely has some ideas that may have a positive impact on the school culture. Use this tool to find or refresh ideas or generate ideas of your own!

My current favorite school or department traditions are:

_____
_____
_____
_____
_____
_____
_____

Which of these opportunities appeal to you? Add additional ideas in the space at the end of the list if needed.

- ☐ Adopt a family for the holidays.
- ☐ Participate in Fun Friday outings.
- ☐ Participate in or conduct a team sporting event (for example, run a 5K).
- ☐ Select an annual charity and collect donations.
- ☐ Celebrate monthly birthdays.
- ☐ Participate in a yoga club.
- ☐ Conduct an off-site team meeting.
- ☐ Provide breakfast or snacks on Mondays.
- ☐ Arrange monthly potlucks.
- ☐ Start a Bring Your Child to Work Day.
- ☐ Conduct end-of-the-semester celebrations.
- ☐ Arrange competitions with other schools or departments.
- ☐ Participate in Wisdom Wednesdays (for example, team members share pro tips).
- ☐ Start a book club.
- ☐ Nominate an unsung hero.
- ☐ Start a Team Spirit Week.
- ☐ Conduct a minigraduation for new educators after the first quarter.
- ☐ Host an ugly sweater contest.
- ☐ Dress like your favorite character from a book.
- ☐ Invite your team to a regular informal after-hours gathering.
- ☐ Host door decorating contests.
- ☐ Celebrate an Employee of the Month.
- ☐ Start a School Spirit Day (by asking students and staff to dress in school attire).
- ☐ Start a Random Acts of Kindness Day.
- ☐ Celebrate International Women's Day.
- ☐ _____
- ☐ _____

CHAPTER 4

People-First Leadership

Real leadership is leaders recognizing that they serve the people that they lead.

—Pete Hoekstra

An acquaintance asked me for one key practice at the iCan Dream Center that supports and sustains my team members through everyday pressures and the occasional crisis, as well as the reverberations from the COVID-19 pandemic. I do not often speak spontaneously and unrehearsed (I am much more comfortable when I prepare in advance!), but what popped out was, "We sacrifice numbers to save people, not the other way around." Put another way, can you think of anything (within your power, of course) you wouldn't do for the benefit of someone you care for, whether it's spiritual, physical, mental, or emotional? This is an ideal mindset for team members to display toward one another.

When I referred to *numbers* in my answer to my acquaintance, I was talking about those items administrators deal with every day. In Illinois, for example, the state promotes a matrix of dates, times, and compliance issues to evaluate schools and leaders. In turn, administrators may adhere to similar systems to evaluate teachers. And sometimes, these requirements are affronts against humanity. Let me tell you a story about how the Chicago Public Schools lost one of their most gifted and dedicated teachers because an administrator chose numbers over people.

Anna interviewed with me for a position as a special education instructor when I served as assistant superintendent for a small suburban school district. She had worked for Chicago Public Schools as a beloved classroom teacher for nearly twenty years, and I knew she was superbly trained. Her references were amazing.

I hired her immediately. What struck me as odd was why Anna had decided to leave her former position after twenty years. People rarely leave Chicago Public Schools for lateral roles after that many years of service. It's a tough job, but the district has great training and excellent salaries and retirement benefits. After hiring her, I asked, "Why did you leave CPS?" Her explanation broke my heart.

Anna had recently sent her daughter away to college. Within the year, she lost her daughter to a tragedy—a victim of on-campus gun violence. Of course, Anna took a leave of absence from her job at Chicago Public Schools. It was several weeks after this tragic loss before Anna returned to her classroom. On her first day back—first thing in the morning—her principal told her, "You're being evaluated today."

Can you imagine that on her first day back? After twenty years and, as she put it, having essentially grown up in this school? This is probably the most insensitive and heartless response I have ever heard in all my years working in schools. This statement communicated to Anna that the evaluation—boxes an administrator needed to check—took precedence over the person on that day (of all days). Anna explained to me she knew at that very moment she had to leave. She worked through the end of the school year, after which I hired her, and she started with my school district.

While the details of Anna's story are exceptional, they illustrate a defining moment—a moment when a dose of compassion might have made all the difference not only to Anna but also to her students. I am certain Anna did not feel like she was a part of her school's work family. Instead, the school and district hurt someone who had given a great deal to them throughout her career, and they lost a great teacher. In chapter 3 (page 41), I described trauma-informed care and its importance to leaders' work in creating a well school culture, as well the importance of moving a step further into trauma-compassionate approaches to leadership. In this chapter, I discuss people-first leadership. Recall from the discussion of the culture of wellness framework in chapter 1 (page 9) that people-first leadership is grounded in serving and empowering others.

What happened to Anna was not people-first leadership. The principal could have advocated to push the evaluation back, providing time for Anna to reacclimate. At an appropriate time, the principal could then alert Anna that an evaluation (in some form) was required. The principal could have invited her into the process of framing what it might look like for her to receive meaningful feedback. This chapter will assist you in understanding the kind of leadership that values serving people and allows you to examine the values that drive your interactions with your team. Elements of servant and transformational leadership philosophies guide people-first leadership. Understanding the trauma-compassionate approach and people-first leadership will give insight and credence to the strategies I offer in chapters 5 and 6 (pages 73 and 95).

Philosophies of People-First Leadership

A significant part of creating a culture of wellness certainly has to do with how you lead. Your own philosophies of leadership and wisdom (that is, your experiences, values, and choices) largely influence how you lead. As a leader, you are responsible for setting the organization's tone (Muhammad, 2018). This is difficult (even impossible) to do effectively unless you demonstrate self-awareness through continuous self-reflection, know your *why*, and consciously lead in accordance with the values that resonate with staff. In this way, you model trauma-compassionate behavior for all and encourage others from your heart.

What you aim to achieve as an educational leader, how you aim to achieve it, and what you leave as a legacy depend on how you build and maintain relationships, communicate, and approach problem solving with your team. Thus, the importance of being aware of your leadership style and which philosophies ground your style are key to the success of your leadership intentions.

Leaders ascribe to different philosophies, which produce a variety of results. The leadership styles in schools play a huge part in the culture leaders create; some are great, some are good, and some are toxic. For example, autocratic leaders, who are inclined to direct and control activities, will often inform their team of decisions they have made with limited or no input from the team. This is not an effective style in developing a culture of wellness. This may result in team members feeling their leader doesn't value their input, thereby undermining team collaboration and innovation. Effective team collaboration is a muscle that leaders need to strengthen; if the leader does not empower the team to collaborate, members could experience atrophy at a time when collective input is imperative.

The ability to recognize needs and adapt to the situation at hand is critical to the success of any leader, and the ability to do this is associated with the style of leadership you exhibit. Most leaders exhibit some principles from one style, while also including practices of another. Figuring out which practices are authentic to *you* is critical; it is an individual process based on your personality, strengths, and weaknesses. This is what makes leaders unique, and the result is what you bring to the table as a leader in your organization.

Several leadership styles are effective in the field of education, and they all have tenets abundant in the people who gravitate to education. "Empowering leadership styles have started to come to the forefront in schools in recent years," (Atik &

Çelik, 2020). Examples include transformational leadership, shared leadership, and democratic leadership. My focus is on the principles of two leadership philosophies that resonate with me as a social worker and an educational leader: (1) servant and (2) transformational. Why? The grounding tenets of both are serving *and* empowering others; the human qualities and values vital for each philosophy are prevalent among educational leaders. Further, the inclusion of self-care and trauma-informed core ideologies within the servant-leadership approach enhance the leader's capacity to transform school culture. Educational leaders are in a unique position to impact the well-being and success of students, teachers, and other related service providers using the blended leadership approach I illustrate in the following sections.

Servant Leadership

Servant leaders put their followers' desires and needs before anything else to increase productivity, performance, and loyalty to both the organization and its leader, which creates stability in teams and positively affects climate and, ultimately, increases well-being for all members of the organization. The philosophy of servant leadership was first recognized as an approach to leadership in business in the early 1970s. This is when Robert K. Greenleaf (1970), one-time AT&T executive turned researcher in leadership and education, published his first essay, "The Servant as Leader," after four decades of studies in the field. Greenleaf (1998) recognized the ineffective authoritarian approach popular during his tenure in a corporate role, and writes that his essay was prompted:

> by my concern for student attitudes which then—and now, although the manifestations are different—seemed low in hope. One cannot be hopeful, it seems to me, unless one accepts and believes that one can live productively in the world as it is—striving, violent, unjust, as well as beautiful, caring, and supportive. I hold that hope, thus defined, is absolutely essential to both sanity and wholeness of life. (p. 21)

Greenleaf's (1998) thought process is affirming. As a leader, you are positioned to restore hope in the individuals you serve. Leaders will never rid their organizations of stress and trauma entirely. However, the strategies and concepts in this book act as a guide to a compassionate and constructive response.

The Greenleaf Center for Servant Leadership published (posthumously) two of Greenleaf's essays on servant leadership, which highlight Greenleaf's (1998) belief:

> As a world society, we have not yet come to grips with the *institutional revolution* that came hard on the heels of the industrial revolution, and that we confront a worldwide crisis of institutional leadership. How can we

ordinary mortals lead governments, businesses, churches, hospitals, schools, philanthropies, communities—yes, even families—to become more serving in this turbulent world? (p. 21)

In his quest to discover how an institution can become more serving, Greenleaf (1998) determined the root of a serving institution is the people who work together as a team toward one common goal, and that work "begins with the initiative of one individual person—no matter how large the institution or how substantial the movement" (p. 22). That individual in your school or district is *you*.

Other theorists emerged who studied Greenleaf's work on the ten characteristics of servant leaders (Blanchard, n.d.; Tait, 2020). These ten characteristics are key for creating the synergy a group within an organization requires to achieve the climate (or environment) favorable to each person's creativity and growth. Ken Blanchard (n.d.), an author and business consultant, believes servant leadership is "both a mindset and a skill set." Leaders require both a commitment to serve and proficiency in applying the principles to positively impact the experience of individuals (*climate*) that result in desirable norms (*culture*) within the organization. The following sections detail my ten principles of servant leadership (adapted from Greenleaf, 1998); the first eight most directly apply when building a culture of wellness for a team, school, or district.

1. Listening

Hearing (n.d.) is the "process, function, or power of perceiving sound." *Listening* (n.d.), however, means "to pay attention to sound; to hear something with thoughtful attention; give consideration." Followers of servant leadership understand the importance of listening as a way of connecting with their team members. *Active listening* includes asking questions, removing distractions, and staying quiet a little longer before jumping in (or listening more attentively). This deliberate approach provides insight and positions leaders to give support that will yield improved outcomes for employees and ultimately the organization (Indeed Editorial Team, 2021).

2. Empathy

A good way to understand *empathy* is to think of it as figuratively standing in someone else's shoes. It's about truly understanding how someone feels and perhaps why they feel the way they do in each circumstance. Servant leadership includes empathy because it can "help leaders better understand their teams and serve them more effectively . . . [even] when you are implementing corrective measures" (Indeed Editorial Team, 2021). Empathy is especially key when executing disciplinary action because while you are rejecting behavior, you are respectful of an individual's humanity (Indeed Editorial Team, 2021).

3. Healing

To perform effectively, a team "must be 'whole' on an individual and collective level" (Indeed Editorial Team, 2021). Educational leaders, especially those working in toxic environments, have the responsibility to create a healing place where members can expect support for their physical, mental, and emotional well-being. Greenleaf (1998) recognized this as early as the 1970s, when he began writing his essays.

4. Self-Awareness

Leaders can never overstate the impact of awareness of how they show up in the world. The Center for Creative Leadership cites *self-awareness* as one of the four fundamental leadership skills (Leading Effectively Staff, 2022). According to Greenleaf, "strong servant leaders can reflect on their own thought processes and behaviors . . . and make sense of the way those things can impact other people" (as cited in Indeed Editorial Team, 2021). Leaders' ability to self-reflect and acquire a sense of self-awareness improves their capability to inspire their team.

5. Persuasion

Leaders who use authoritarian approaches to leadership like providing orders, directives, or otherwise trying to convince team members to comply and conform, neither inspire nor motivate. "Instead, [servant leaders] use persuasion to convince others to agree with their decisions and take action accordingly" (Indeed Editorial Team, 2021). A shared approach to leadership in education provides higher satisfaction among educators (Atik & Çelik, 2020).

6. Stewardship

Stewardship refers to the careful and responsible management of something entrusted to one's care. For example, in the case of a financial adviser, *stewardship* refers to the management of someone else's money. In the case of planet Earth, one might feel that stewardship of this shared environment is everyone's responsibility. "Stewardship is the way we carry out this entrust; it focuses on the fact that we aren't the owner—merely the one responsible. Servant leaders are conspicuously aware that they don't exercise control, rather they exercise influence" (Shoff, 2020). In the case of educational leaders, stewardship of their employees and students is their responsibility. Recognizing each person's importance to an organization is a cornerstone of servant leadership. According to Greenleaf, "each member of an organization carries some responsibility for the stewardship of the organization" (as cited in Indeed Editorial Team, 2021).

7. Growth

This key principle of servant leadership "emphasizes the intrinsic value of each team member. As such, servant leaders usually find it important to support their people's growth and development" (Indeed Editorial Team, 2021). Being aware of, thoughtful about, and attentive to each person's professional needs and aspirations is key to demonstrating a leader's commitment to the growth of the team and organization. Servant leaders are unwavering in their belief that each person has "something to offer beyond their tangible contributions" (Barbuto, 2007). Understanding an individual's needs and aspirations relates directly to the importance of developing relationships and connecting with those in your school.

8. Community

Who wants to spend time in a place where they don't feel valued? Whether at home, a restaurant, school, or work, the answer is probably the same: *no one*. Servant leadership emphasizes the benefit of building community because it "honors team members' intrinsic value and can support their performance by helping them feel valued" (Indeed Editorial Team, 2021). "Getting the job done is not enough. Servant leaders are also concerned about the health and strength of the team and the overall sense of community presence throughout the organization" (Laub, n.d.).

9. Foresight

Foresight is the ability to apply learning gained from previous situations. Committing to the process of reflection to make meaning of experiences is powerful for leaders. "Foresight also sometimes relies on intuition, and it can be useful to notice that sense as well" (Indeed Editorial Team, 2021). This is beneficial in all leaders and ties to self-awareness. School leaders can reflect on recurring situations to determine how they developed in their responses and applied knowledge as a starting point for reflection.

10. Conceptualization

Conceptualization is the practice of developing solutions for broad organizational challenges. This is an asset because it positions leaders to direct their team according to the core values and mission of the organization. Conceptualizing requires discipline and practice to "think beyond the day-to-day realities" (Spears, 2010). Educational leaders who master conceptualization become critical to the school district or organization.

School districts and other nonprofit organizations are moving from hierarchical leadership to more empowering leadership styles, which has increased teacher satisfaction (Atik & Çelik, 2020). The ten principles of servant leadership not only give power and voice to team members but also value them beyond their professional contributions. Servant leadership is a people-first approach because it honors the humanity of each person.

Transformational Leadership

The second leadership philosophy that resonates with me is *transformational leadership* because its foundation rests on discovering what your teachers and staff members need, then empowering them so they can move the organization forward by creating and innovating in ways you may have never even thought about. It is critical to this book and the framework for a culture of wellness because the goal of transformational leadership is to shift organizational culture to something better for all members.

Author and leadership studies authority James MacGregor Burns introduced the concepts of transforming leadership and transactional leadership in his 1978 book, *Leadership*. The key difference between the two, he explains, is that "transforming leadership is a process in which leaders and followers help each other to advance to a higher level of morale and motivation" (Burns, 1978, p. 1). Transactional leaders, on the other hand, don't normally seek cultural change and instead work within the existing culture (Burns, 1978).

In an article on dynamic leadership, coauthors A. Gregory Stone, Robert F. Russell, and Kathleen Patterson (2003) discuss servant and transformational leadership and determine that at the heart of transformational leadership is the leaders' focus on expanding the interests of those they lead in favor of rising above their own self-interests for the good of the mission and purpose of the organization. If you apply a transformational leadership scenario to Anna's situation from the beginning of this chapter (see page 57), the principal would have advocated to supervisors to delay the evaluation in favor of supporting a grieving teacher. Note that the principal would take this action even at the risk of an unfavorable response. The result may have been increased stability for the students, school, and district because Anna would have felt supported and valued rather than the need to seek new employment.

Researchers expanding on the concepts of transformational leadership theory identify four elements (*Four* Is) that others recognize as the fundamental leadership behaviors of a transformational leader (Khan, Rehmat, Butt, Farooqi, & Asim, 2020; Korejan & Shahbazi, 2016). The following four behavioral elements work together to build an environment that enhances follower commitment, transcends follower self-interest, and empowers and motivates followers to pursue the organization's vision.

1. *Individualized consideration* is essentially leaders ensuring their followers' individual professional needs (including professional development and advancement) are met. Leaders provide mentoring, coaching, challenges, and support to team members. The idea behind individualized consideration is to ensure leaders inspire their followers to make contributions to the team while maintaining professional goals of their own.

2. *Intellectual stimulation* is how leaders inspire creativity, innovation, and independent thinking in pursuit of problem solving and progress.

3. *Inspirational motivation* happens when leaders articulate the organization's vision to their followers so it is attractive and provides a sense of purpose. According to Stone and colleagues (2003), "The transformational leader builds relationships with followers through interactive *communication*, which forms a cultural bond between the two participants and leads to a shifting of values by both parties toward common ground" (p. 3).

4. *Idealized influence* occurs when a leader consciously acts as an authentic role model for valued behavior, which inspires followers' pride, respect, and trust.

The Four *I*s of transformational leadership are reflective of people-first leadership. The assumptions of servant leadership and transformational leadership are similar in that they both highlight the value of the people in the organization and the importance of appreciating, hearing, supporting, and guiding followers while instilling trust, credibility, and respect. The primary difference between the two is where the leader's focus resides. "The transformational leader's focus is directed toward the organization, and his or her behavior builds follower commitment toward organizational objectives, while the servant leader's focus is on the followers, and the achievement of organizational objectives is a subordinate outcome" (Stone et al., 2003, p. 1).

People-First Leadership and the Framework for a Culture of Wellness

The transformational and servant leadership styles resonate with me because both provide a positive, achievable purpose for creating the environmental adjustments leaders need to protect and preserve their teachers. These styles also prevent burnout and compassion fatigue in service providers while supporting the organizational vision of better outcomes for students. These leadership philosophies are invaluable for school leaders invested in the educators they serve. The behaviors inherent in servant and transformational leadership function together as a people-first approach; people-first leadership with the trauma-compassionate approach form the framework for a culture of wellness (see figure 4.1).

Figure 4.1: People-first leadership and the framework for a culture of wellness.

Motivating and supporting school personnel in a way that creates a safe and supportive learning environment for students will result in positive educational performance and outcomes. I developed a tool to align with people-first leadership to support and sustain positive outcomes. It is based on the well-known SWOT analysis, which is a structure that provides for the examination of strengths, weaknesses, opportunities, and threats (Tanner, 2020). I offer a SWOP analysis (strengths, weaknesses, opportunities, and plan), which I find more effective in mitigating the brief time schools allot for school teams to plan, operationalizing the responses to identified pain points, and moving toward action. This is a great tool for reviewing new initiatives, considering revamping practices, and for ongoing quality assurance to ensure optimal performance and operations. See the reproducible "SWOP Analysis" (page 71).

Chapters 5 (page 73) and 6 (page 95) present actionable strategies born from the trauma-compassionate approach and people-first leadership. Now that you have information about the significance of their aspects, you will learn how to apply the strategies that converge to create a culture of wellness. The strategies in chapter 5 focus on school, department, or team leadership. The strategies in chapter 6 focus on the organizational level, with the goal of developing an overall culture of wellness (rather than pockets of wellness within the district or larger organization).

Please use The Culture Within section to further explore the contents of this chapter through the lens of your own experiences, values, and perceptions.

The Culture Within

How intentional are you in your rapport-building actions and communications as you move throughout your day?

Which aspects of servant leadership and transformational leadership resonate with you most? Why?

Reflect on a time when you were the beneficiary of people-first leadership. What did it look and feel like? How might you replicate some of the most inspiring examples of people-first leadership that benefited you?

_____
_____
_____
_____
_____
_____
_____
_____
_____
_____
_____
_____
_____
_____
_____
_____
_____
_____
_____
_____
_____
_____
_____
_____
_____
_____
_____

SWOP Analysis

In the SWOP analysis it is important to identify the time frame and objective of the analysis (for example, first semester science fair, district hiring practices, climate in the middle school) so everyone has the same scope for reflection.

Objective: _____ Time Frame: _____

Strengths	Weaknesses	Opportunities	Plans
What are the outcomes we want to replicate? What is going well? What positive feedback did we receive?	What needs adjustment? In what ways was there underperformance? What was the negative feedback?	What are the specific opportunities for improvement? What are the threats to future success? Which stakeholder can we include to enhance outcomes?	Write a specific, measurable, and attainable goal relevant to the identified opportunities. Does the goal address a weakness? Does it leverage strengths?

CHAPTER 5

Team Leadership

The most effective way to do it is to do it.
—Amelia Earhart

I was working in my office one afternoon when I received a phone call from a woman who had recently taken on the challenging position of director of student services in a neighboring district. This was her first leadership role (a remarkably substantial initial role), and someone suggested she call me for help. It was 2010, my third year as director of special education. I had gained some state board of education recognition for my program designs and the overall improvements in services for neurodiverse learners within the district.

I said, "Absolutely" and shared with her what I knew about all the different reports from the state, the time lines, and what she needed to focus on immediately. I shared with her my approach to team meetings and staffing structures; she was trying to build a program similar to one I had developed to support students with behavioral and emotional needs in my school district. I appreciated the direction in which her school district was moving, so I didn't hesitate to assist her. I invited her, the district psychologists, and her other key team members to join our meetings so they could see what data points to examine to make decisions.

In essence, this developed a mentorship. I shared many hard-earned lessons. However, I believe the most critical components I shared were about leading in a way that is people first and trauma compassionate. Fast forward over a decade, and she is now assistant superintendent in the same district. I regularly interact with her team, who gladly serves alongside her. Together, they continue to provide phenomenal service to vulnerable students. The small role I played has informed the work of other leaders and resulted in student success.

The key understanding of this experience is what an immeasurable reward leaders can reap (for themselves and others) with just a little extra effort. Leadership is demanding, but the degree to which your actions and their effects can ripple out into the world in such positive and impactful ways is rewarding beyond measure. Those ripple effects often occur because of changes you make at an organizational level (a topic I will discuss in chapter 6, page 95), but whether you lead at a department, school, or district level, never lose sight of how your decisions affect the team members you work with and depend on every day.

Consider for a moment who is on your team. A *team* is a group of people who join to perform a common activity. You may have chosen your team members, or you may have inherited them. They might be your direct reports, which could exist at the department, school, or district level, but in any context, the group's common activity remains to ensure the success of students and staff. What does the culture look like inside your team? Regardless of who makes up your team, the goal is to transform the culture within to reduce and perhaps prevent the outside stress and chaos from overwhelming your team members. Thus, it's important to have some strategies at your disposal to help you achieve this goal with your team members.

The trauma-compassionate, people-first strategies educational leaders practice are different from showing up as you might as a parent or a partner. Leadership must be authentic. You can best achieve authentic leadership with a mindset of being a compassionate and transformational servant of those you lead while respecting the professional boundaries inherent among workplace colleagues—you can't exactly send a colleague for a sensory break! However, I adapted this chapter's team-leadership strategies from the same ideas that underpin proven trauma-informed instructional practices teachers use to show up for their students. These strategies align with what educators know about how best to serve individuals affected by ACEs, as well as the principles of servant and transformational leadership that many authentic and self-aware leaders already inherently practice. These are the most salient strategies in educational environments as leaders work toward institutionalizing a culture of wellness in their schools at the team level. The strategies I share are designed for the team level because the leader implements them. The strategies represent a shift in a leader's approach rather than policy changes. The strategies give credence to this shift.

To that end, this chapter is about the following actions that will yield rewards.

- Creating connection
- Being present
- Checking in first
- Creating structure
- Building community
- Infusing choice
- Utilizing think time and processing time
- Guarding emotional safety
- Respecting time away
- Paying it forward

These actions inform the team-level strategies I developed and used to transform school culture when I worked in public schools, and the strategies I employ at the iCan Dream Center. I do not list the strategies in a prescriptive order. To be effective, your use of them will be as unique as your organization.

Stress and chaos aren't going away, but with a heart full of compassion, you can fend off stress and chaos. Doing purposeful, little things can yield big transformations in your team. For example, I often have team members comment on how much it means that we celebrate each member's birthday and publicly acknowledge achievements such as marriages and earning new credentials. It requires some coordination and about five dollars for a card, balloon, and a printed sign, but it does so much to affirm my team members, which is powerful beyond measure. Remember: when you feel overwhelmed—and you will—the best way to keep moving forward is to start small and just keep moving in the direction of positive change one step at a time. Step by step, you will build relationships and support structures that counterbalance the stress and chaos of your everyday life and environments. Your teams and students deserve it!

Create Connection

One of the most important and best deterrents to burnout and compassion fatigue is connection (Theisen, 2021). Connection is one of the most essential values within a trauma-compassionate learning organization because the number-one resiliency factor for anyone who has experienced trauma is to feel connected to others and have a sense of belonging. When educators (or people in general) talk about resiliency factors, connection is always number one. To give this gift of connection takes an investment of time. There's no replacement for it. What, then, is *connection*?

Think of it as the opposite of *small talk*—that often short, inane chatter that exists between people who really don't want to be in the same room. Personal connections are made through interactions that have depth and meaning, but not everyone is going to connect at high levels. The goal as humans is to connect to the extent possible. At the very least, connect so you understand where the other person is coming from; being best friends isn't the target. When meaningful connections are made between people, it's difficult to discount or dislike someone, and compassion and grace flow more freely during the more difficult times.

How do people make these connections? An example that might be familiar is one teachers and school social workers use with students called *check and connect*. In the example (IES, n.d.) that can be found at this web address, https://ies.ed.gov/ncee/wwc/EvidenceSnapshot/78, in which an interventionist implements check and connect as a dropout-prevention strategy, it's the end result that exposes how connected the interventionist is with students. When teachers aren't seeking to connect with students because their mindset is that they *have to* go through this check and connect because they're going to get evaluated on it, then it's just a box they check. It only indicates, "Yes, I met with a student. Yes, I went through the steps that I was supposed to."

When reviewing data for multi-tiered systems of support with my team at one of my former workplaces, we quickly realized that teachers were just checking boxes, and we didn't see any changes for students; no connections were being made. When our teachers, practitioners, and social workers were genuinely and authentically connecting with students, we found those students soaring! The difference in these student outcomes was simply the connection the students felt with teachers who care for, watch over, and inspire them.

I think this same principle bears out when it comes to leaders supporting teachers. The magic is in the mindset of the leader and in the personalization of the connection between the leader and the team member. Remember, it's an investment of your time. How you decide to connect really doesn't matter. It can be making eye contact and genuinely inquiring about the team member's weekend. It might be having a cup of coffee together. Just remember to ask questions (about work or not). Make it less about you and more about them. Use your curiosity and compassion. It is possible you are not inherently interested in connecting with your team, which will mean making a connection is tougher. However, you may have to treat the effort like some treat writing reports; put it on your to-do list, because it is a requirement if you desire a culture of wellness.

Team members must feel like they want to perform for you, their leader. You can gauge the strength of their desire by the amount of resistance from your team. Team members should see your attention as reinforcement, and they need to know you care about them. They want you to see them working hard. There's no magic in checking in without the genuine compassion and caring that goes with it. Start small. Start with one person and connect.

Be Present

A team leader said to me once after a meeting, "I didn't notice any of that stuff! You always know what's going on!" I don't recall the subject, but I do remember my response. I said, "That's not a good thing. Are you too preoccupied to tune in to people's body language, their facial expressions, their nonverbals, and what they're not saying? That's not a badge of honor, it is a sign that you are doing something else other than being present."

Everyone suffers from not being present at times. They might be bored, busy, hurting, or just not practiced in the art of being present. But *being present*—fully conscious of the moment you are in, free from internal thoughts and dialogue—is essential when working with people (particularly with those who have experienced trauma) and making connections with them.

When leaders are not present for each member of their team, people cannot connect. In fact, when leaders are not present, the opposite happens; people disconnect, and it's difficult to establish or recover relationships once this occurs.

To *be present* is to ensure you are listening with empathy and giving your full attention. A study finds cultivating presence is incredibly beneficial in coping with single and multiple stressful events (Donald, Atkins, Parker, Christie, & Ryan, 2016). When your teachers, who are potential trauma survivors, can be present with your support and modeling, they are more productive.

The key to this strategy is the ability to take a moment to pause and do what you need to do so you can truly be present in a moment. It may take some practice to be present in one moment, particularly if you are inclined to multitasking or rapid switch-tasking. Take a moment to reflect and ask yourself, "How can I prepare myself to be available?" It can be as simple as taking a deliberate step to not fidget with your phone while you're in a meeting or having a conversation. You will know you are present in the moment when you focus on what is occurring, aware of your body and emotional state, and fully engage—when your mind is not anywhere else. For leaders, part of the importance of the be-present strategy is also to model being-present behavior for others. Commit to being present in the workplace and mentally ready, just like you expect your teachers to show up for their students.

Check In First

It's obvious when a student enters a classroom and isn't ready to learn. The student's attitude, appearance, behavior, or performance might reflect this unpreparedness. In the realm of trauma-informed care, the teacher's willingness to check in first with the student, then recognize and respond to that student's immediate needs first before proceeding, is an acknowledgment of the student's humanity (Burch, 2019).

Trauma-informed care with students prescribes a check-in first practice, which might sound like this: "How was your weekend?" or "How's your morning?" The practice continues with a visual scan for signs of anything left unsaid and concludes with a response to that student's immediate needs in an effort to clear the student's mind to receive the next thing. According to blogger Jenna Buckle (n.d.), this practice is effective in gathering information regarding a student's state of mind and gaining insight on how best to assist the student for optimal classroom performance. Because they haven't necessarily developed the coping skills or self-awareness to know what is mentally percolating in their backgrounds, educators must discern if the students are prepared to learn.

There is more onus on adults to articulate their mental states and to be more self-aware. As a leader, you don't know what your team comes with through the door on any given day. For example, take an adult whose partner yells at him every morning before leaving for work. When the adult arrives, he is probably not in the optimal place for work performance. So even for adults, an initial check-in is an important strategy. But it looks a little different. Ask questions like the following.

- "Is this a good time to meet?"
- "How are you?"
- "Do you have the mental bandwidth to discuss . . . ?"
- "How was your weekend?"

As you develop and strengthen your connections with each team member, the questions you ask may become more personal.

A friend and colleague used this check-in practice with me just as we were preparing to meet. She simply asked, "Is this a good time?" I had just learned that one of my good friend's closest friends had passed away unexpectedly. So *no*, it wasn't a good time. But the simple check-in practice enabled me to acknowledge all the emotion just beneath the surface. Ironically, I had not given myself permission to cancel that meeting. I was grateful my colleague insisted we reschedule. I spent thirty minutes weeping for my friend's loss, gathering myself, and composing a note of encouragement to my friend. Ironically, my colleague and I were meeting to record a podcast. I cannot imagine the outcome had we moved forward. When we connected to record a few weeks later, it was phenomenal and one of my best interviews to date.

When someone is not present to receive what you're saying, the conversation is futile. People must be at some level of equilibrium to process what they are doing. In the preceding personal example, my colleague recognized I had "checked out," then inquired and confirmed I was not in a space to receive what was coming next (the podcast interview). She acknowledged my humanity with compassion and understanding. Checking in first is an amazingly powerful and underestimated strategy.

Create Structure

Structure often translates into safety in the classroom (Meador, 2019). Give people a sense of control by letting them know what they can expect and anticipate. A sense of control is useful for people who may or may not have had that anchor in the past or in other parts of their life. Predictability is also especially beneficial for people who have experienced trauma. If you create predictability in their work environment, people will gain a sense of control and a clear vision of what to expect. When people know what to expect, they perform better. This is no different for the people you lead. Leadership researcher Brené Brown (2018) notes, "Clear is kind. Unclear is unkind."

I have a healthy appreciation of structure. As a type A personality, I approach things with the intent of making everything clear; typically, I plan out things well. I share an agenda a few days in advance so people know what the meeting will be about and can prepare. After the meeting, I prepare a summary so people have a record of what occurred. However, when conducting our weekly meetings, I missed this glaring, obvious *thing* that my team needed to know to better carry out their work. What did I forget? Ready for this? I completely missed assigning tasks and completion dates to outstanding items! Let me give you a quick example.

During one meeting, my team decided it would ring a bell to cue the lunch transition. Well, who's going to ring the bell? What kind of bell is this person going to ring? When is the deadline for implementation? My team had multiple pieces to this seemingly simple task and needed the dates I was expecting for implementation and other information so they could decide how to prioritize the task. How could I miss this? I had zero structure for assigning tasks during my staff meetings. I realized it may have looked as though there was clarity and structure (in my own mind at least), but people left the meeting confused and lost. It was my staff's feedback that clarified this oversight. My team then begin using a chart to add clarity. See the reproducible, "RACI Board" (page 94).

To prepare my staff for changes, new projects, and other items that require communication via meetings, I provide structure. These are simple practices that yield clear pathways forward with well-defined expectations for *who*, *what*, *when*, and *how*. It is my expectation that leaders do the same for their teams too.

First, I prepare and send an agenda at least a couple of days ahead of the meeting to give people time to think about the content and process it a little bit beforehand. See the "Meeting Agenda Planner" reproducible (page 93). The agenda can change the entire atmosphere of a meeting. A common response I get when I ask my team leaders to prepare and send out an agenda ahead of time is "That's just one more thing to do." However, I encourage the practice by noting it will make meetings more effective and a better use of their time.

Second, I send minutes out to everyone immediately after the meeting. I stress the word *immediately*—meaning when the minutes are relevant, not three or four days later. Meeting minutes do not have to read like a novel. In fact, *brief is better*. Just include the highlights and action items from the meeting (what the team needs to accomplish, by when, and by whom).

Finally, I introduce new concepts, processes, procedures, and so on as much as possible during a meeting versus via email. If it is a new concept or a new approach, I need to discuss it with my team in person. You need to look people in the face, read their confusion, and then give them a chance to ask questions and receive clarification.

Another benefit of meeting to discuss new items is that even if it's a new practice you think is airtight, once people start asking questions and making comments, what you thought was straightforward may not be. I learned this the hard way; I thought I knew a process, but I learned from my teammates I was missing a step or two. So, the discussion should occur in person. Use email to document and reiterate what the team shared, perhaps addressing a lingering question from the in-person discussion.

Build Community

While *connection* is about knowing someone cares about you as an individual, is invested in you, and lets you know you are significant, a *community* represents the place where you belong—your people. For people to be their best, they need to feel a sense of belonging, and this is especially important to those who have experienced trauma, a difficult time, or just an overwhelming moment. According to the blog of the Kenzie Academy from Southern New Hampshire University (2020), "The healthiest and happiest modern workplaces have strayed from the cold, corporate feel and are offering employees the opportunity to build community with their teammates."

When working within your own team, community building as a trauma-compassionate leadership strategy gradually creates a sense of belonging among the members. Many school districts do this well, but often take the impact for granted. There are some simple ways you can build community, including acknowledging birthdays, having celebrations, and socializing. But remember, building community must be deliberate.

During one of my leadership workshops, I asked the participants for some examples of community building. One workshop participant shared her story, which had a bigger impact than she initially expected.

She explained she would give a candy bar with a little celebratory printed note to team members on their birthdays. She said it was just a small thing, but she would always put the items on the team members' desks first thing in the morning, so the gesture greeted them when they arrived. She said she never thought much about it; it was just something she did.

After she left that district, she'd occasionally reconnect with those she left behind. (Ahh . . . the power of connection!) She noted one consistent comment her former colleagues made to her was about missing this small act of birthday acknowledgment and kindness; the succeeding supervisor did not pick up this tradition. It's the little things—like candy bars and printed notes—that let your team members know you see and appreciate them. Therefore, it is no surprise research substantiates that most people entering the workforce place a great value on the sense of community (Clutch, 2018). If not birthdays, celebrate something else. At the iCan Dream Center, I give a five-dollar gift card to anyone who provides an example of someone else demonstrating one of our core values in action, which leads people to attend to one another.

Even if there are effective community-building strategies at the organizational level, it's important to build community in your team, department, or school because each team within an organization is different. The differences result from the leadership, connections, and community-building those teams accomplish.

Utilize Think Time and Processing Time

Think time and *processing time* are cousins to the creating-structure strategy. Both allow your team to process information ahead of time for the benefit of discussion, increased productivity, and accountability. *Think time* is the time prior to performing the next step in a series, while *processing time* refers to the actual time spent on a task. Think time and processing time are important because they allow people to organize ideas, strategies, and communication with other team members. Also, intentionally providing think time and processing time to survivors of trauma or ACEs helps them integrate thoughts and feelings. I think everyone needs this time.

Can you think of a situation more stressful than having little or no time to process a response that could mean the difference between winning a million dollars or losing everything? How about a job interview? Sometimes even responding during a team meeting can be an anxious time for some. Think time and processing time are beneficial for everyone, especially people who get stressed under pressure and require time to process ideas, thoughts, and responses. According to a course at the Harvard Graduate School of Education (2023), think time increases confidence. At the iCan Dream Center, my staff and I distribute agendas ahead of time to give team members time to process and prepare their responses and contributions. Those most needing think time and processing time may not give adequate feedback if the meeting is the first time they've heard of the subject. My best example relates to job candidates.

Think about the time and expense it takes to hire someone for a position, not to mention the time you and your colleagues spend in front of those candidates. Ideally, you want to hire the best candidate in the least amount of time, right? To help them prepare for the interview, I give all candidates the interview questions ahead of time, just before the interview. Yep! I give them all the questions. So, while they're waiting, they can look over the questions, prepare their thoughts, and think about how they want to structure their answers. And the earlier they arrive, the more time they have to review. I find this practice decreases a candidate's stress and increases the thoughtfulness of their answers. As a result, it provides interviewers with more information with which to gauge a candidate's fit for the position, not how well they perform—or not—under pressure. Some additional ways to use think time and processing time with your teachers and staff are as follows.

- When team members request to meet, ask them to prepare an agenda to frame their questions. This requires they set aside time to formulate thoughts and articulate their needs. Receiving the agenda prior to the meeting allows leaders think time to ensure their time is meaningful.

- Open your leadership team meeting with a prompt. Ask your team to spend two to five minutes responding in long hand. This processing time allows team members to think deeply, be present, and (by journaling) help their brain to regulate emotions. Thoughtful, present, and regulated is an ideal state of mind to begin a meeting.

- Set up think time at the end of each day for your entire school team. Leaders could dismiss students ninety minutes prior to the instructional staff. This allows time for daily collaboration, planning, and innovating. While you may not have ninety minutes in your school schedule, most teachers have planning time, which in the best-case scenario they should use for think time and processing time.

Infuse Choice

When people have more control over their circumstances, situations, and decisions, they tend to feel more invested (Atik & Çelik, 2020). *Infusing choice* is the strategy of giving people ownership in the decisions that involve them by inviting them to be participants in decision-making processes when possible. Where there is consent, choice, and contribution, there is buy-in and community building. This is applicable to all people, but it may be especially vital for those who have had ACEs.

A common attribute among those who've suffered trauma includes feeling a loss of control (Hancock & Bryant, 2018). This stems from what was happening during the time the trauma was inflicted; trauma survivors were the recipients of others' decisions. Create a *biome* for your teams—a place where people don't feel like things are happening *to* them, but rather where they're positioned or invited to choose and give their consent when feasible, and as frequently as possible.

Here's an example: the dreaded lunch schedule. It's a simple thing. Educators know they need a schedule that articulates who will provide lunch supervision to students. It's quite simple for the leader to just plug in names. It's quick too. But imagine how much buy-in you would get if you did it that way and left out choice. Little or none, I'd say. But, if you asked people about their preferences for scheduling, even though it takes more time and effort to figure out fifteen slots (and I know that's not a lot—some of you have twice that number!), it is worth the effort. It's more cumbersome than if you just wrote names in slots. But the additional time it takes may yield big results as an investment in your team, even if you cannot fulfill all requests. Perhaps the lunch schedule isn't the place to infuse choice in your organization. But look for chances to infuse choice where you can. It's a small thing, but it yields big results in your investment in your team. It's about inviting your team to participate.

Guard Emotional Safety

Do you recall the CDC's (2020) first principle for a trauma-informed approach from chapter 3 (page 41)? It's *safety*. It's easy to fall into the trap of thinking only about school and student safety when considering safety: fire drills, weather emergencies, vandalism, and student fights, to name a few. However, leaders must recognize that safety in a team encompasses so much more. This strategy focuses on ensuring the environment in which the team works feels both physically and psychologically safe for everyone. While physical safety concerns can be easy to identify and address, psychological safety is a bit trickier. Some of the biggest threats to psychological safety are general relational aggression, gossiping, and isolating a target. Guarding emotional safety requires combating those conditions and behaviors. I discuss these three issues in the following sections.

Address Relational Aggression

Relational aggression is the nonphysical form of bullying and often occurs via manipulative or controlling behavior. I once heard it referred to as "hitting with feelings." And because relational aggression is purposefully subtle, it's easy to miss. But it can do substantial harm to people and a school's environment. The following story is one of the most subtle instances of relational aggression, and it happened to me.

At the time of this incident, I was the director of special education, and the woman involved, while not my direct supervisor, was an assistant superintendent. Helen charged herself with collecting contributions for a retirement gift for a fellow colleague. When Helen approached me and asked if I wanted to contribute to a "tennis gift," I declined. I knew the retiree loved to fly Southwest Airlines and I said was going to get him a Southwest gift card which was, at the time, new to the market.

Several days later, at the retirement luncheon, everyone got up to present the group gift. Helen got up in front of everyone and said, "We all thought it was such a good idea!" The group gift was a Southwest gift card. And there I was, separately, with my little individual gift card. Helen had purposefully diminished my contribution. I sought her out afterward and said, "Why wouldn't you either, one, ask me to contribute to the new gift, or two, tell me you guys had shifted from a tennis gift to a Southwest gift card?" The response? She simply looked at me and kept moving.

How do you address something like this with a colleague? Should I have mentioned this to the superintendent? It would feel like tattling; "She did this!" Silly, right? What's the superintendent going to do about it? This was an admittedly small, but habitual, type of behavior from this colleague, but enough of those little instances can take a toll on someone, especially someone who's not working in an emotionally safe environment.

While it primarily affects adolescents, nonphysical bullying (and other forms of relational aggression) can and do occur at any age, and they can occur in the workplace. As leaders, we must call out this type of behavior as soon as it is observed or reported, address the aggressor directly, and celebrate team members publicly who are contributing positively to the culture.

Stop Gossip

I think it's worth saying: schools can be gossipy environments. Watercooler and coffeepot conversations can be so disruptive and toxic to an organization (Syntrio, 2021). I'll tell you a story without any context.

A local administrator was seen touching the stomach of a pregnant woman in a hallway at school.

What's your first thought? What's your first reaction?

The gossip mill went into high gear, and in no time at all, word around the building was that the married administrator was expecting an outside-of-marriage child with this woman. The truth was the woman was a relative of his whom he hadn't seen in a while. To be fair, they had not disclosed their relationship due to his leadership role within the district. But the person who noticed the incident—someone with no context nor business related to the people involved—decided to deliver a tale to the first available listener. It could have destroyed both of their careers; you can't always reverse that kind of harm.

Guarding emotional safety is such a focal point within the iCan Dream Center, and one important way I ensure it is to directly address gossip. I bring the importance of this up during interviews. During a review of our organizational values with each newly hired candidate, I expound on the point that at the iCan Dream Center, we do not accept any gossip. If someone is talking about something that has to do with someone else, and the person talking has no power to change it, it's gossip, period. If someone talks to someone else about a situation that has nothing to do with them, it's gossip. And if they don't have permission to share, then they shouldn't be talking about it. I can't think of anything more polarizing than an environment where people feel excluded because of gossip. Yes, sometimes stuff slips through the cracks, so in your role as leader it's imperative you deal with that gossip swiftly and unambiguously to avoid any unpleasant consequences.

Prevent Isolation of a Target

Another especially hurtful type of relational aggression is *isolating a target*. I started to realize that a little clique was developing within my organization. Those involved were deliberately alienating other team members, and the target seemed to move from one person to the next. I reiterated frequently my expectations to the senior team member involved in the clique, to the point that I referenced it in an evaluation document. The last straw was a particularly infuriating group text. The clique targeted a person who wasn't aware of a historical fact and sent a group text to everyone to make fun of this person's lack of knowledge. I pulled two team members aside, and said in no uncertain terms, "I know what you're doing. It's rude. It's hurtful. And it's bullying behavior. Anytime you're going to put something somewhere so that everybody can laugh at (not with) another person, it's not OK, and it doesn't work here."

The final thing I said was, "This will be an environment where people feel included and not excluded." Ultimately, employment was severed with one of the team members involved. On her final day, the team—even those who had been hurt by her actions—celebrated her contributions to the organization, and she was released with my blessings.

Many things can make an environment feel unsafe for someone; it's up to you to recognize what those things are and interrupt it. For example, as a leader, it would be wise to observe interactions among team members, note typical seating arrangements and changes therein, attune to who is most inclined to proffer feedback and who reserves comment on certain topics, and observe body language (for example, hand wringing, shifting in seat, reduced eye contact, and shared gazes). Body language such as this can single hostility or warmth, exclusivity or inclusivity, and, of course, a sense of ease or fear. Respond as needed to what you observe.

Respect Time Away

Are your employees scrolling through their emails looking for that message from you after work hours, on the weekends, or during their vacations or holidays? Do you receive replies outside regular work hours?

Imagine if your organization banned emails after work hours. Would you feel relief, or would you see this as an obstacle to your ability to get work done? Early in 2016, France passed a labor reform bill that outlawed employees from accessing emails on the weekends (Lehigh University, 2016). The reason behind the ban is a study that connected organizational expectations for employees to respond to emails after hours and exhaustion (Lehigh University, 2016). The study succinctly concludes, "'off' hour emailing . . . negatively impacts employee emotional states, leading to 'burnout'" and implicates it is the expectation (not the actual time spent on the emails) that drove the resulting exhaustion (Lehigh University, 2016).

People who never fully disconnect from the workplace suffer from burnout and, further, when they do work during their time off, it undermines a critical factor that determines whether people persist happily in their work: *intrinsic motivation* (Giurge & Woolley, 2020). According to educational psychologists, activities that provide an inherent satisfaction, rather than an external reward, mark intrinsic motivation (Ryan & Deci, 2000); it is why many educators spend the hours they do working. However, when people feel expected to work during their off times (which, of course, undermines inherent satisfaction), it creates an internal conflict because they are supposed to be enjoying personal time (Giurge & Woolley, 2020).

When people are somewhere other than work, it's indeed time away, but if they're still doing work or communicating about work, it's not disconnecting from work. Part of the support educational leaders must provide includes respecting team members' time off. This includes parental leave, vacation, sick days, holidays, evenings, and weekends. I admit I am guilty of sending a quick text message or email at times when team members are off. But as a practice, I do not schedule critical messages to go out after work hours. If you want your team members to show up creative, energized, and innovative, it's imperative that you hold sacred the time and space they need to recharge.

A culture that praises and expects an always-on mentality prevents employees from unplugging and perpetuates the stress and chaos which ultimately lead to burnout and compassion fatigue. It's up to educational leaders—*you*—to turn off the always-on mindset and let your employees disengage when they're away from work.

Pay It Forward

To *pay it forward* refers to acts of kindness or doing good deeds for others versus paying someone back for a good deed. Buying lunch for a guy on the side of the road, holding the door open for a person with a physical disability, or giving a stranded driver a gallon of gas are all ways people pay it forward. People see small acts of kindness toward strangers all the time. Why do they do it? They might not see the results of their good deed. Maybe that lunch was the first meal that guy had in two days. Maybe this is the person's first day using a walker. Maybe that gallon of gas got a family to an emergency care center just in time. You may not know. Maybe the recipients were grateful, maybe they were not. Does it matter? I say *no*. The result is that you were making someone's circumstances better than they were before you got there. Perhaps it stirred compassion and generosity in others. Acts of kindness can also affect the culture and climate at home and work.

My personal philosophy is that paying it forward is just a good thing to do. For me, compassion and paying it forward create a broader sense of community, a sense that "we are all in this together." When people take care of others—strangers or not—it trickles down and expands. And while the purpose of an act of kindness should never involve what it can do for the giver, a lot of times, it comes back to the giver. Within the context of trauma-compassionate leadership strategies, one of the principle ways to pay it forward is being willing to mentor others. This is particularly important to me as a woman of color in leadership. And for me, I'll say that a really a big part of where the iCan Dream Center staff is today is because of my willingness to pay it forward.

Remember the assistant superintendent I mentioned mentoring at the beginning of this chapter (see page 73)? We formed a very solid, collegial relationship. Prior to opening the iCan Dream Center, I built a transition program for a public school district. She reached out and asked if she could send students from her district to my school district's transition program. My superintendent said, "Absolutely not."

Within weeks of receiving approval from the state board of education for the iCan Dream Center, this same colleague's district was the first to enroll students. She knew firsthand the quality of my work and my laser focus on students and outcomes. And even today, the center has a continued relationship with her district, one of three dozen partner school districts.

Who knows what kind of seeds you're going to plant? I didn't. I couldn't imagine those next steps. But what I did know was I wanted my colleague to be successful. She had a district full of students she needed to serve well, so I jumped in to help and support her.

Paying it forward as an educational leader is intentionally being willing to help people who want to be in leadership. For me, as a woman and specifically as a woman of color, it's important to assist in overcoming certain barriers when you can. If you have some insight to help someone to break a barrier, then you should. Why not? There are enough seats for everyone at the table.

My last words on this? Find someone to mentor and pay it forward!

These are the ten strategies educational leaders can implement as they build their own cultures of wellness within their team, department, or school. To some, these strategies might feel small, not enough to make an impact at all. Others might see these approaches as a raindrop in the ocean: "Is any of this going to even make a dent?" I assure you, they will. These intentional trauma-compassionate leadership approaches can be the difference between a collaborative, healthy, productive team working within a culture of health and wellness, and not.

Making small changes one step at a time may make you feel powerless, like your sphere of influence is too small because there are bigger constraints out there at the organizational level. You want organizational change now, right? But change takes time, patience, and small steps. If you are able to make bigger changes and contribute to or have influence at higher levels within your organization, districtwide changes and beyond are not off the table, as you will see in chapter 6 (page 95).

Please use The Culture Within section to further explore the contents of this chapter through the lens of your own experiences, values, and perceptions.

The Culture Within

Which strategy in this chapter resonates most with you right now and why?

Is there a strategy from the chapter that feels challenging to you—how so, and how might you address those challenges?

Identify someone you might mentor. How else might you pay it forward?

Meeting Agenda Planner

Use this example meeting agenda plan to develop an agenda for your own meetings with your staff. Having a consistent format will help you ensure you cover all the necessary items in your plan and provide structure.

Add your organization's logo at the top of your planner template. Providing the logo automatically unites people with a shared purpose.

Opening Prompt: Use an opening prompt. This could be a motivational quote or question or statement designed to prompt reflection on the organization's values, goals, or accomplishments. Share a student success story from this past week.

Starting the meeting with a point of reflection gives team members a chance to connect through sharing. It's best to choose a prompt that is positive and provides the opportunity to celebrate accomplishments. Ask team members to spend two minutes journaling their responses before sharing.

Opening Pro Tip: Include a quote or blurb that enhances the skill set of your team. For example: "Effective leadership is putting first things first. Effective management is discipline, carrying it out." (Covey, 1989)

Agenda Item #1: Fall quarter professional development

- Action item
  Select dates
- Action item
  Select presenters

Distribute the agenda to team members one to three days prior to the meeting so they are prepared to meaningfully contribute.

Agenda Item #2: Science Fair

- Action item
  Suggest committee members
- Action item
  Discuss relevant resource vendors

Agenda Item #3: Offer roundtable time.

Agenda Item #4: Provide time for team members to acknowledge one another.

Create a window of time for open conversation, brainstorming, and creative problem solving.

Clarify the next meeting time.

11/10, 2:00 pm

End your time together by giving each team member an opportunity to recognize others. This ensures the team members look for the positive contributions of others, and it feels great for colleagues to recognize fellow team members.

Set up your team for success by reminding them of important dates. This is a placeholder for reminders, not the initial announcement. Share initial date announcements verbally to allow space for discussion.

Source: Covey, S.R. (1989). The seven habits of highly effective people: Restoring the character ethic. New York: Free Press. Source for logo: ©2022 iCan Dream Center. Used with permission.

RACI Board

Use a RACI Board to plan tasks for your team. This tool is particularly useful for team projects that require input from various sources. Hang this chart in a visible location or place it on a shared online platform all team members can reference.

Write tasks in a SMART goal format (Conzemius & O'Neill, 2014).

Responsible? = Who is assigned the task?

Accountable? = Whose final approval is required?

Consulted? = Whose input is required for successful execution?

Informed? = What stakeholders need to be informed upon completion? Who needs progress updates?

Task Due Date	Who Is Responsible?	Who Is Accountable?	Who Should Be Consulted?	Who Should Be Informed?

Source: Conzemius, A. E., & O'Neill, J. (2014). The handbook for SMART school teams: Revitalizing best practices for collaboration (2nd ed.). Bloomington, IN: Solution Tree Press.

CHAPTER 6

Organizational Leadership

> The things we fear most in organizations—fluctuations, disturbances, imbalances—are the primary sources of creativity.
> —Margaret J. Wheatley

A friend who had recently accepted a superintendent position asked me to breakfast. The gathering was a celebration of his new role and an opportunity to confidentially share his concerns. Most relevant to me was the condition of the student services department. It lacked a leader for various reasons, was absent a true continuum of service, was marked by toxicity and low student expectations, and was battling multiple lawsuits, to name just a few issues. Shortly after our breakfast, I conducted a thorough needs assessment. My feedback to my friend was, "The lawsuits are all legitimate. If I were those parents, I would have taken legal action as well," and "All hope is not lost if you commit to sustaining the pressure that comes with much-needed change."

It was like he was sitting in a room with a blindfold over his eyes. I entered the room and changed the landscape. Often, when change is needed, leaders don't have a clear understanding of what is required to lead change. Leaders cannot see clearly, yet they know things are shifting. I shared the *what* and *why*, and my friend and I worked with all stakeholders to craft the *how* to fix it together. The superintendent, school principals, related service providers, and teachers felt deeply vulnerable, however, because certainty about an outcome can feel safer than uncertainty—even when that uncertainty may encompass movement toward positive change. Their choice could have been to turn and run, but instead they took my outstretched hand without reservation, and they bravely moved forward.

Eventually, my consultant role with that organization became a permanent one. I committed to only two years but remained for five to ensure stability for the staff, students, and families whom I still carry in my heart.

You might not think you can have an impact at the organizational level, but you can. If you work through your uncertainty and fear, institutionalizing a culture of wellness is within your ability. This chapter will provide strategies to improve organizational culture. I will discuss toxicity and how to impact change in service to your teachers and students.

Fear of Change

Change nearly always brings with it uncertainty, and with uncertainty comes fear and stress. People deal with fear and the uncertainty of change differently because everyone has different tolerance levels. There are the "Heck, yes!" people who approach change with an open mind and heart for the greater good. There are the "Maybe . . . I'll stick a toe in and see how it goes" people who need convincing, and then there are those who will turn and run, shouting, "But we've always done it *this* way! I'm out!"

Neuroscientist and author Marc Lewis (2016) conducted a study on uncertainty and concludes, "all measures of stress, both subjective and objective, maxed out when uncertainty was highest." So people feel more stress when they speculate about the *possibility* of something negative happening; for example, they feel more stress if they feel reasonably certain of getting fired, whether or not they're going to (Lewis, 2016).

You may ask, "Why would anyone choose the certainty of a negative outcome over the uncertainty of knowing it's a possibility?" Because human brains are wired to hate uncertainty (Razzetti, 2018).

But despite the human brain's proclivity to resist uncertainty and opt for the known (whether good or bad), brains are adaptive and trainable; people have choices (Razzetti, 2018). People can let fear get in the way and lose sight of what is possible, or they can choose uncertainty, face the fear of the unknown, and thrive in change (Razzetti, 2018). You've chosen to move forward and thrive. That's why you're still reading this book, right?

Why does this matter? Because institutionalizing cultural change is not for the faint of heart. As you've seen, it takes time, thought, intentional effort, and one small step at a time. It's a difficult undertaking. As the quote at the beginning of this chapter from author Margaret J. Wheatley says, leaders can overcome the fluctuations, disturbances, and imbalances within organizations to inspire creative and innovative solutions for change. Leaders are the ones who push through the uncertainty and fear of change, and inspire solutions. After leaders work through uncertainty and fear, they must help their colleagues push through their insecurities and trepidation.

In chapter 5 (page 73), I looked at the team and how various strategies have the capacity to change the culture, or perhaps the subculture of your team. I say *subculture* to differentiate the culture within a leader's team or department from the culture of an entire school or district, that is from the culture of the organization as a whole. I differentiate between these two levels because the focus of the strategies is different for each. Both sets of strategies (at the team and organizational levels) are required to institutionalize a culture of wellness, and in many cases, as a leader, you will deploy both types of strategies. The following two points illustrate the differences between team-level and organization-level strategies.

1. **Team-level strategies focus on building relationships and support structures within your team or most direct circle of influence:** In essence, these strategies are representative of what functional family members do for one another. They counterbalance the stress and chaos in the immediate environment. For example, at the end of a tough, stressful day, you can walk into your home and family members will surround you, putting their arms around you and comforting, supporting, and listening to you. A strong team with a positive, supportive culture in the workplace does the same thing.

2. **Organizational strategies focus on changing culture by reducing or preventing stress and chaos in the whole organizational workplace and implementing policy-level changes:** This is at the heart of designing and institutionalizing a culture of wellness within an educational organization. Organizational strategies further transform the climate and culture of an organization in ways that prevent stress and chaos from occurring at toxic levels.

People, coworkers, and family members alike will always need comforting arms for life's adversities and tragedies. The goal of employing organization-level strategies is to mitigate the need for those emergency comforts. Or at the very least, reserve that comfort—those metaphorical benches in the bathroom—for well-deserved rest rather than for escape. There are as many strategies for organizational change as there are creative leaders to dream them up. In my quest for institutionalized cultural wellness, I've identified the following strategies as being the most helpful when building an organizational culture of wellness.

Identify Toxicity Within an Organization

Conflict among personnel, manipulation, unethical conduct, bullying, harassment, lack of recognition, little or no collaboration or communication, insistence on policy over people, hurtful gossip, and so much more mark toxic environments. Toxic educational environments have high employee-turnover rates, low morale, fear, sinking productivity, and stressed-out teachers.

While some are blessed to work in positive, supportive learning environments, many teachers and administrators are not. In some instances, an entire organization might be toxic. In others, toxicity may only exist within a subculture or two inside the organization. In either case, the danger is that these suboptimal environments can impede and even prohibit progress within an organization. Multiple studies correlate the health of a school's culture directly to student outcomes as well as to an organization's ability to innovate and improve (Deal & Peterson, 2016). When a district's toxic culture prohibits the ability to move forward and change, the ultimate losers are the teachers, staff, and students.

Acknowledging and identifying a toxic environment within an organization is vital to changing it. Acknowledge and call out toxic behaviors every single time they surface. Doing so requires a commitment from the entire executive leadership team of central office staff.

When leaders allow toxic environments to fester, students are the ones who suffer, the very people educators are called on to serve. Studies suggest that paying attention to a school's culture is one of the most important responsibilities of educational leaders and fundamental to teacher morale and student achievement (Deal & Peterson, 2016; MacNeil, Prater, & Busch, 2009).

To assist in identifying toxic cultures, Deal and Peterson (2016) identify common characteristics of toxic cultures in school environments in their book, *Shaping School Culture*.

- **Individuals are focused on self-interest:** There is little concern about the impact of decisions on students, families, or the surrounding community.
- **System operates in fragmented silos:** Teams, departments, and schools have their own approaches, with limited or ineffective communication to improve overall district operations.
- **The atmosphere is hostile and destructive:** Teams are generally negative.

- **Informal network is filled with secretive people:** People conduct lots of hushed conversations and hoard information and insight.

- **Retaliation is the common way to deal with disagreements:** Retribution is frequent—even for offering differing perspectives.

- **Students are treated as burdens, and ideas, materials, and solutions are rarely shared:** People regard students as "the problem" and consistently do not value or share strategies to support them and address challenges.

- **Apathy and dissatisfaction are common:** Little effort to innovate is evident, as are low expectations for students; complaints abound.

- **Few positive rituals or ceremonies that unite people:** There is no sense of belonging outside cliques.

- **Misuse of public social media platforms:** People use Facebook, Twitter, and other platforms to embarrass others through attacks, complaints, or criticism. Social media is an outlet for exposing negativity.

I've seen some pretty toxic behaviors in my leadership roles, and I've seen administrators turn a blind eye to them. On one occasion, while working in higher education, I was admonished for calling out a blatant inconsistency. I was told to resign if I didn't like it. I took that recommendation!

In another school environment, the administrator's approach to toxic scenarios was, "This is not happening! You guys should all just get along!" This response resulted from his discomfort with conflict. (It's OK to be uncomfortable with conflict, but that doesn't mean you pretend it doesn't exist.)

A superintendent once told me he *wanted* to let the toxicity continue because, in his mind, it was survival of the fittest. It was like fighting on the playground: whoever survives, survives. He refused to address toxic behavior and infighting. I was in utter shock. The weird thing about this? I have tremendous respect for this leader. But I could not disagree more with his stance on toxicity. (It's possible to disagree with a colleague's position on a subject but still have a positive relationship and connection.)

The key to subduing toxicity is to immediately and consistently recognize it (that is, *name the unacceptable behavior*), with your entire executive leadership team in agreement. Once your team has explicitly identified toxicity, remind the offenders their behavior is unacceptable and intolerable. This stance allows wellness to permeate the organization. However, the rules for this behavior can't be different from one department or attendance center to another, nor can an administrator choose to call out one person, but then let toxicity fester in others.

Create Space for the Human Experience

There's a theme running through this book about the importance of relationships and connection. The concept of creating space for the human experience within your organization is congruent with this theme. Let me explain.

By definition, *human experience* is a term for the countless realities of human existence people encounter within the mental, emotional, spiritual, and physical realms of life (Spacey, 2018). All people share common experiences: birth, time, childhood, sickness and pain, fear, freedom, happiness, aging, mortality, and yes, work, to name a few. While most people share these experiences, it's important to note they process them differently. People's perspectives are not always the same. That's part of what makes each person unique, and why some people face change with an open mind while others turn their backs.

I am going to summarize a well-known account best-selling author and speaker Stephen R. Covey (1989) introduces in his book *The Seven Habits of Highly Effective People* because it clearly illustrates the importance and need to create spaces in the workplace to allow for shared human experiences.

Covey recalls a paradigm shift when he encountered a father on the subway with his children. The kids were "loud and rambunctious" but the man seemed oblivious and closed his eyes, yet the children altered the experience of the other riders by tossing objects and yelling (as cited in Sage, n.d.). Covey's irritation increased and finally he asked the gentlemen to take notice and intervene. The father responded, "I guess I should do something about it. We just came from the hospital where their mother died about an hour ago" (as cited in Sage, n.d.). Understandably, Covey's feelings changed instantly, his rage was replaced with empathy and compassion (as cited in Sage, n.d.).

While no one intentionally created the space where this shared human experience changed Covey's perspective, the experience did alter the way he saw and felt about it to the extent that it altered the way he behaved—with more grace and compassion. Covey realized there is always more to the human experience than what people see on the outside (as cited in Sage, n.d.).

So how does this revelation relate to creating space for the human experience in a work environment? Healthy work relationships are critical to well-being. Maslow's hierarchy of needs illustrates that "after physiological and safety needs have been fulfilled, the third level of human needs is social and involves feelings of belongingness" which encompass social necessities like relationships, connectedness, and belonging (as cited in Mcleod, 2022). This is what creating space for shared humanity is about. Leaders create time and space where people can relate to one another and get to know one another as human beings. Then, during the workday, people see beyond just what's in front of them—like the quiet man and his rambunctious children on the subway (Sage, n.d.).

It's the leaders' role to seek out and create as many shared experiences within the workplace as possible, because most people, especially in the workplace, don't seek them out. The environment should offer spaces, literally and figuratively (as in contexts and activities) where people can come together and let others inside where it's not forced, it's not weird—it's where people can be their authentic selves.

Public school districts approximate this approach with gatherings for staff, such as holiday and retirement parties. (This is the lower-hanging fruit on the tree of approaches.) During these events, people try to have fun, but it's difficult to get past the perception that *it's still work*. People try to tell themselves and perhaps one another, "Hey, let's turn off work for a bit and have fun." But the extent to which people are really going to be "letting their hair down" and having a genuine good time is based on the tone leadership sets.

Picture this: you're at a holiday party. You're sitting at a table, but still in full work mode, still thinking and talking about work. You don't really know what to say. You worry about saying the wrong thing. You just can't engage socially because it's still work, right? When people observe their leaders remaining "on" during work-related social events, they aren't going to feel free to enjoy themselves and connect on a human level, which is entirely the point of creating these spaces.

It's plain and simple: creating space for the human experience is intentionally creating time and place for nurturing and supporting the social connections among those with whom you work. Getting rid of this always-on mentality is essential. The space and environment should invite people into positive relationships where they can share the human experience. When people get to know one another, their stress decreases, and their health and performance increase. Maslow's third level in the hierarchy gets fulfilled (as cited in Mcleod, 2022).

Work relationships can be just as meaningful and celebrated as relationships outside work. Once they've built this awareness about one another through sharing human experiences, loyalty, grace, and compassion abound even when the workday isn't perfect. It's the leaders' job to ensure people in the organization know leaders do not expect them to always be available for work outside work hours.

In my last school district, staff did a not-always-on operational mode exceptionally well. In fact, I still go to their events! They still call me, and I'm the one who attends their leadership retreats just for the fun parts. That's a testament to the successful relationship building that took place when I worked there. With the not-always-on philosophy, there was a clear line of demarcation. In that district, the attitude was "work hard, play hard." When the work was over, staff always had a good time going to the karaoke microphone, sports events, and the like.

I adopted part of that culture for the iCan Dream Center to ensure my staff really get to know one another, so they learn to work well, play well, and be well together. It's OK to disagree with someone's approach to something, but it's hard to dislike someone you've come to understand through shared experiences. The additional insight you gain from sharing your human experiences gives you another perspective—you understand where the others are coming from. Like Covey (1989) and the man on the train, you begin to see inside the people with whom you spend a large part of your workday. It takes trust, connection, and transparency, which sharing the human experience fosters.

Hire for Zeal

My business coach posed a question about *zeal* as it pertains to my team at the iCan Dream Center. He wanted to know if my team members exuded positive energy, eagerness, and fervor in their daily tasks. Though this was not an area I had explored heavily, I assured him the overwhelming majority of my team members had zeal to spare. I could state this confidently because their zeal had been evident during their hiring interview.

When hiring, I ask questions that get to a candidate's heart for the students. I request stories that assess their passion, empathy, and commitment to young people. Philosophically, I believe you can teach people effective instructional practices, but it is impossible to teach them how to care for others, much less how to connect with their purpose in the world.

This approach has been beneficial in identifying and hiring ideal candidates across educational settings including higher education, public schools, and a therapeutic school. Screening for heart and soft skills (over hard skills) has yielded positive outcomes for the iCan Dream Center. This is not to say that practitioners who are zealous or passionate about their work do not experience burnout. Life can throw curve balls, but when your work clearly aligns with your purpose, the toughest day at work can feel like a respite from the difficulties in your personal life.

I have taken some missteps. I can think of a couple of times I hired because I needed a person to fill a role quickly. Both times, I failed to consider the impact having people who struggle in their roles could have. I found myself coaching, encouraging, and motivating them often. For both new hires, there was a disconnect with where staff were as an organization. The rest of the team saw these two as outliers. Culturally and organizationally, I never wanted anyone to look to them as models of our organization. What an arduous, defeating, and isolating situation for the employees as well.

In short, it's about hiring the right kind of people for your organization. In his book *The Ideal Team Player*, organizational health pioneer and author Patrick M. Lencioni (2016) describes his model, which simplifies the soft skills ideal for the team player into three virtues: (1) hungry, (2) humble, and (3) smart.

- *Hungry* implies the person possesses a strong work ethic, is a contributor, and applies determination to complete the mission.

- *Humble* means exactly that—there is little ego and lots of focus on service to others versus service to self.

- *Smart* does not mean book smart. It implies emotional intelligence, the people smarts by which people understand themselves and others, know how to communicate and work cooperatively, are internally motivated, and possess compassion and empathy.

The approach here is that while hard skills are important, it's the soft skills that enable leaders to best provide for students and collaborate with peers. This is what leaders should be screening for when hiring. Leaders who hire employees who already demonstrate humility, hunger, and smarts get better results and eliminate politics, turnover, and morale issues (Lencioni, 2016). The next question is, How does a leader screen for these qualities and ensure there's passion for the position?

The interview process is key. Develop questions that access passion, hunger, humility, and smarts. While the questions on the surface appear standard, screening for these qualities requires you to listen closely to what the job candidates share and do not share. Make the decision to press until you receive a response that reveals the individual's heart.

For example, I want to know if a candidate easily admits to mistakes. One of the inquiries I usually include during an interview is to have candidates tell me about a time they made a mistake. Follow-up questions include, "How did you handle that?" and "What would you do differently?" I don't really care what the mistake was; I want to know if candidates (1) can reflect on their own behavior, (2) have thought about how they can continue to grow as an individual and a professional, and (3) can acknowledge their own imperfections.

Educators must acknowledge that most administrators will not have the opportunity to select their entire team. In cases where team members are already in the organization, it is critical to place them in roles that align with their gifts and training.

For example, in special education, when a student is not performing or behaving in a productive way for learning, a team assesses whether the student has a performance or skill deficit and then develops a behavior support plan. Similarly, educational leaders deal with employees who are underperforming. By asking questions, leaders can develop plans to maximize employee output. I often ask myself when tailoring support, "Is an employee not performing because he, she, or they lack the skill, or does he, she, or they lack the motivation to consistently execute the skill?" This approach can put you on the right track when assessing a current employee who is underperforming in a current role and might be a better fit in another role.

The reason the hire-for-zeal strategy pertains to the entire organization is because hiring for zeal must come from the top down and be consistent across all departments throughout the organization to be effective. Additionally, since it is common for educators to change roles, departments, or schools, even if hired for one area, the team member is an employee of the organization.

Interviews are difficult; even when done correctly; not everyone can conduct a good interview. You must ask the right questions and interpret the answers, both of which are entirely dependent on the organizational culture and nature of the position. Currently, in addition to me, there are only two people at the iCan Dream Center who conduct initial interviews. I've had to train them to recognize and listen for soft skills. Ensure you and your hiring team assess for the right qualities, not for what potential employees look like on paper, their technical abilities, or hard skills. Do this by assessing the person's passion, hunger, humility, and smarts, and how well the person will fit in with the culture of wellness you have or seek.

Encourage Vacations

The United States' reputation as a nation of workaholics is well known. Even the Center for Economic and Policy Research has gone so far as to call the United States the "No Vacation Nation" (as cited in Castrillion, 2021). This is not a surprise, but did you know:

> [In 2018] American workers left a record number of vacation days on the table—768 million days, up 9% from 2017. Of the unused days, 236 million were forfeited completely, equating to $65.5 billion in lost benefits. More than half (55%) of workers reported they did not use all their allotted time off. (U.S. Travel Association, 2019)

Additional studies find the following.

- Twenty-six percent of respondents had never taken two weeks of vacation at one time (Castrillion, 2021).
- Americans work an average 184 more hours per year than the Japanese, 294 more hours than the British, and 301 more hours than the French (Miller, 2023).

What excuses do Americans have for not using vacation time? While you might think the "perpetrators of this crime" of lost, forgotten, and ignored vacation days are Wall Street executives, bankers, entrepreneurs, CEOs, and doctors, school leaders are guilty too. Consider the consequences of neglecting vacations:

> Leaving vacation time on the table is taking its toll on employees. A recent study by the World Health Organization (WHO) found that 745,000 people died in 2016 from heart disease and stroke due to long [work] hours. . . . The research found that working 55 hours or more per week was associated with a 35% higher risk of stroke and a 17% higher risk of dying from heart disease than a workweek of 35 to 40 hours.
>
> Taking vacation time is essential to employee survival. That's because time off from work is integral to well-being, sustained productivity, and high performance. . . . some additional reasons to start planning your next getaway. (Castrillion, 2021)

Other reasons include increasing your mindfulness, improving heart health, lowering your stress, boosting your brain power, and enhancing your sleep (Castrillion, 2021). Emma Seppälä (2017), an international speaker and a lecturer and director at Yale University, notes, "Research suggests that leisure is an important predictor of our well-being and satisfaction with life, including our health, work engagement, creativity, and even marital satisfaction." She continues, "for people of all ages, leisure activities like visiting friends and family and going to church are positively linked to well-being" (Seppälä, 2017). Research shows "that inability to detach from work comes with symptoms of burnout, which of course impact well-being and productivity" (as cited in Seppälä, 2017). Seppälä (2017) adds:

> Disengaging from work when you are not at work . . . makes us more resilient in the face of stress and more productive and engaged at work. Even a short weekend getaway can provide significant work-stress recovery, while longer trips away provide even more relief.

Extended staycations at home with no work also provide this relief (Seppälä, 2017).

Retooling the culture of neglecting vacation time, regardless of the industry, is controversial. I know this because I have worked where there is a strong culture of buying back vacation days. I had fifty-six vacation days on the books when I left my last job. At the time, I was happy to take the money, pay off my car, and take myself on a trip. But in retrospect, it probably would have been better if I'd taken a vacation now and then. I'm smarter about that now.

I understand the educational industry is different, and consistency in the classroom is important. Most administrators work a twelve-month calendar, but some organizations expect both administrators and teachers to work their 180 days and schedule vacation time during the summer months and other holidays throughout the year. Sometimes, educators save vacation time and personal days, which leads to the propensity of turning vacation and personal days into sick days, which can turn into early retirement. Encourage your school leaders to take their vacation time. Encourage teachers working a nine-month calendar (with summers off and more breaks throughout the school year) to take personal days as needed. In addition to encouraging people to use their vacation time and personal days, another organizational approach might be to limit the number of days an employee can buy back.

Educational leaders must fight for what is healthy and beneficial for themselves, their teachers, and their students. The research provides enough evidence to encourage educational leaders and teachers to use their benefits to get away, recharge, and return ready to get back to work. If regular breaks and time off from work make better leaders and teachers—that is, more present, less stressed, and healthier—why wouldn't leaders advocate for the full use of vacation and personal days for their entire team?

Ultimately, David W. Ballard, who heads the American Psychological Association Center for Organizational Excellence, says it best:

> People need time off from work to recover from stress and prevent burnout. . . . Websites and magazine articles offer plenty of tips on how to make the most of time out of the office, but often put the onus on the individual employee and ignore important organizational factors. A supportive culture and supervisor, the availability of adequate paid time off, effective work-life policies and practices, and psychological issues like trust and fairness all play a major role in how employees achieve maximum recharge. . . . Much of that message comes from the top, but a culture that supports time off is woven

> throughout all aspects of the workplace. (as cited in American Psychological Association , 2018)

Again, many educational organizations limit the number of days and the specific times of year teachers and administrators can take days off for good reason. This is where I believe administrators must get creative for change versus doing "what we have always done." If leaders don't step outside the education business comfort box, they will never move their organization forward toward improved wellness.

Include Wellness in Collective Bargaining

This strategy builds on the strategy of encouraging vacations by addressing the critical nature of time away from the workplace to enable people to disengage and recharge. This is a separate strategy from the encourage-vacations strategy because it requires a decision leaders cannot make unilaterally—or even with school board approval. Using a strategy to include wellness in collective bargaining must involve teachers.

By way of full disclosure, I have not personally seen this strategy in action in a public school system; I have only experienced it at the iCan Dream Center. But my extensive experience sitting on the management side of the bargaining table tells me that creative changes to the school calendar can solve several issues related to both teacher burnout and student achievement.

Most districts must adhere to a minimum of 180 school days in a calendar year, so there are limited days during which administrators can take vacation and teachers can take personal time. Organizations limit the time and number of days off in favor of increased benefits inside the classroom. To be clear and transparent, the iCan Dream Center does limit the days its teachers can take off because it is a school and teacher presence and consistency are beneficial to both students and teachers.

Nonetheless, it's up to leaders to ensure enough breaks throughout the year because teachers and some administrators cannot take a vacation during the school year. I mitigated the issue of limited time off by incorporating a four-day weekend every month (two in March because it's a long, dreary, cold month in the Midwest) and a five-day minivacation each quarter. Yes, it makes the school year a bit longer because my school is still subject to the same minimum number of school days as the public schools, but my choice to redesign the annual calendar increases both our students' and teachers' well-being (Zubrzycki, 2015). To be clear, I am not necessarily suggesting year-round schooling, but rather adding ten to twenty days to the standard calendar to accommodate intermittant breaks.

This approach comes with two other benefits as well. First, students' summer break is shorter. Studies show the *summer slide*, where student knowledge retention from the previous year diminishes over the course of long summer breaks, is real. A study followed students in grades 1 through 6 over five summers and concludes that over those summers, 52 percent of students lost an average of 39 percent of their total school year gains (De La Rosa, 2020).

Additionally, teachers often spend a good chunk of time in August reviewing and refreshing students on the skills they learned the year before. (This is why many students perform better at the beginning of the year!) I think my students' knowledge retention (shortened summers reinforce this retention and minimize the summer slide by opting for more frequent breaks throughout the year) is worth the effort to change the calendar.

Teachers traditionally work August to June without vacations. Yes, they do get the same holidays as the students, but teachers often work outside the school day on extracurricular activities, meetings, grading, lesson planning, tutoring, and so on. Teachers barely get bathroom breaks during the day. In sum, I think it's worth a discussion to incorporate more breaks throughout the school year. Staff, teacher, and student well-being benefit from well-placed breaks throughout the school year.

The previous research suggests that overall health declines as the number of hours worked per week rises. So it makes sense that incorporating more frequent breaks throughout the school year—three- or four-day weekends—can provide a pause in an always hectic school year to allow teachers to recuperate monthly.

As a leader, you know the school calendar has a lot of moving parts, such as input from the unions, parents, and community. Implications to changing the school calendar might include pushback from parents' places of employment. Even though they might philosophically agree that teachers need breaks, these employers also might feel it's too inconvenient to coordinate their work schedule or to change how they approach child care to accommodate a nontraditional school calendar.

I also understand some educational systems will not condone having their leaders take all their vacation days. And there are some educational veterans who just don't take vacation days because that's "the way it's always been done," or they feel taking vacation days is "a sign of slacking." These thought processes are based on the idea of a strong work ethic that frowns on people taking their vacation time.

Among the moving parts of the school calendar are negotiating contracts, agreeing on them, and then approving them. There are ways to overcome the obstacles to change, but it will require tenacity and perseverance to accept slow changes. My point here is that there are different ways to think about the calendar, and leaders should push for organization-level benefits to increase wellness—like more breaks during the school year—instead of "doing what we've always done."

Give Staff Permission to Engage in Self-Care

Remember the opening story about the benches in the bathroom (page 1)? It was a proactive, compassionate board member (and retired teacher) who acknowledged the need for a bench in the bathroom. Administrators who authorized the installation of the bench also acknowledged they value self-care and wellness for their teachers. The bench in the bathroom amounted to permission for the teachers to engage in self-care.

One final strategy you can employ to institutionalize wellness within your organization is to ensure all executive leaders are onboard and *loudly* give permission for all within the organization to engage in self-care and wellness activities.

How is this done? As I mentioned previously, there are many ways organizations can contribute and encourage wellness. Some can be relatively low or no cost, like walking or participating in yoga clubs, water-drinking competitions, FitBit or iWatch competitions, meditation rooms, and even music. (Just think: you can create spaces for the human experience at the same time!) Also, it's important to promote opportunities and programs that include activities for all areas of wellness: physical, spiritual, mental, and social.

When researching other organizations' wellness programs, I found many that are world renowned. (Note: many of these types of programs are in corporate settings.) Some companies—Google, Huffington Post, Ben & Jerry's—to name a few, even sponsor on-the-job sleeping, and they have nap rooms! (Kaprál, 2018). But what's good for one organization isn't always good, or even viable, for another. For schools, educators know budgets and schedules are at the forefront of squeezing other priorities into a work or school day. It's a matter of getting creative with what you've got.

It's worth saying that organizations do not have to sponsor, initiate, or sanction all wellness programs. When employees engage in their own wellness activities (like adhering to a morning routine or regularly exercising on their own time), these activities are just as beneficial and organizations can also celebrate them.

Within the educational environment, I discovered a few activities that are simple to initiate and can work wonders for stressed-out teachers—everything from participating in running groups to taking line dancing classes. Chief among them is ensuring an opportunity for staff to say, "I'm overwhelmed at the moment, and

I need a bit of a break." A five-minute walk might make all the difference. I've seen it work. In a school culture where five-minute bathroom breaks are nearly unheard of, this might be a stretch, but it just might make all the difference to a teacher in that moment.

The types of wellness programs and initiatives that fit within your organization's personality, time, and budget are up to you and those who participate. The following are two elements all successful wellness initiatives have in common.

1. Unwavering support and encouragement from the leaders, who give permission to engage in wellness activities
2. Open and constant celebration for those working toward wellness

Celebration includes reinforcing the wellness practices you see. And as I mentioned, creating space for your staff to say, "I'm not OK" and enabling them to take that break encourages wellness at its most basic level. Inspiring these practices sometimes requires direct inquiry. As the leader, start the conversation. Ask, "What are you doing to care for yourself?" Let your staff know you see them taking care of themselves and applaud them for it.

It's important to differentiate between the recognition of wellness routines or practices and what I would consider a one-off, like participating once in a water-drinking contest. That's not to say leaders shouldn't reward or recognize participation, but please note the difference between the two. Leaders want staff participation in meaningful and continuing wellness routines. I have two team members who take lunch at the same time every day and do laps around the building during that time. I let them know that I see them and highly approve of them doing this. It's a life change for many to engage in these types of activities.

Educators hear a lot about corporate wellness programs because those are the ones that make the top-ten lists and get mentioned in magazine articles. Schools, however, not so much. But just because schools don't have the same budgets as corporations and must work around student learning and schedules doesn't mean wellness programs aren't worth the time and effort. They are! In the end, you're going to have a better team, department, school, and district when your staff members are moving their bodies, drinking water, eating healthy, taking the time to reflect, and having moments to themselves. You *can* create a better environment for employees who will then show up better for the students.

Circling back to where this chapter began (with the emotions of uncertainty, and sometimes resistance, to the possibility of change), how would you respond to making the changes described here? How would your teachers respond? How would you lead?

Change in an organization is scary for everyone. For leaders, it can be especially scary because they see the magnitude and the level of difficulty of the change required. And leaders like you are responsible for its success or failure. But remember: a leader cannot change an organization alone. Changes that take people and their organizations outside their comfort zone require leaders who lead with trust and transparency and team members who are willing to change.

As an effective leader, it is incumbent on you to develop an implementation plan. The reproducible "Wellness Initiative Planning Checklist" (page 117) is designed for districts and schools with no prior experience with employee wellness initiatives, as well as for those seeking to improve an existing initiative. Using this tool is a great starting point for the selection of strategies, timing, and processes you must plan based on your organization's unique profile. Organizational changes take time, and the results will depend on this context. However, committing to these strategies will make the transformation less daunting, and create buy-in as you move toward a school culture of wellness.

In the next chapter, see how leaders at a real-world school in California used many of the strategies this book supports to develop a strong, inclusive culture that fosters growth in both staff members and students.

Please use The Culture Within section to further explore the contents of this chapter through the lens of your own experiences, values, and perceptions.

The Culture Within

What strategies in this chapter resonate with you? Why?

Is there one strategy from the chapter you could apply to take a first small step to better the culture of your organization?

How do you think your colleagues might approach a culture change? How can you plan to address barriers that fear imposes?

Hire for Zeal Interview Questions

Each question has a specific objective. It is imperative to employ active listening to hear what a candidate may not explicitly state. Avoid *yes* or *no* questions, and follow up with a request for specific examples when a candidate makes broad statements. Tune in to body language.

Note: This is not an exhaustive list of interview questions, but rather some prompts that will allow you a glimpse of a candidate's passion, people skills, and humility after you determine the candidate has the requisite qualifications for the role.

- Tell me about your path. How did decide on a career in _____? (Objective: This will give you a sense of what the candidate is truly passionate about, such as contributing or money.)
- What is an example of a time you took on lower-level work for the good of the team? (Objective: This will help you gauge the candidate's humility and willingness to sacrifice for the overall team.)
- When was the last time you apologized in a professional setting? What was the circumstance and how was the apology received? (Objective: This will help you determine the candidate's willingness to admit mistakes. Watch for body language and superficial examples.)
- In your current role, what does it look like to exceed expectations? How does what you describe characterize you? (Objective: This will help you determine if the candidate believes operating in excellence is "above and beyond." You will also get a sense of the candidate's passion for work and sense of responsibility for the team's success.)
- What is an example of a time you relied on your intuition about a situation rather than simply the facts? What was the outcome? (Objective: This will provide insight into the candidate's emotional intelligence.)
- What is an example of a time you disagreed with your supervisor's feedback? How did you handle it? What would you do differently in the future? (Objective: This will help you gain insight on the candidate's ability to humbly receive corrective feedback, handle conflict, and adjust behavior.)
- How do you define diversity? What is your experience working in diverse environments? (Objective: This will help you determine the candidate's feeling about people different from the candidate and the candidate's preparedness to make meaningful connections. Listen for problematic responses like "I treat everyone the same," "I am colorblind," "I have a friend/neighbor/cousin that is _____, so I know all about it.")
- Would others describe you as an attentive listener? Why? (Objective: This will help you gain insight into the candidate's emotional intelligence.)
- What is an example of a time you personally celebrated a team member? Did you initiate or plan the acknowledgment? (Objective: This will help you determine the candidate's ability to see other people's accomplishments. This is a measure of emotional intelligence and important to maintaining a positive culture.)

- What makes you most excited about your new role? Most nervous? (Objective: This will provide insight into what areas the candidate feels confident and where you can plan to provide extra support, coaching, and reassurance if you select the candidate for the position.)

Source: Adapted from Lencioni, P. M. (2016). The ideal team player: How to recognize and cultivate the three essential virtues—A leadership fable. *Hoboken, NJ: Wiley.*

Wellness Initiative Planning Checklist

If you have any of the following in place, you are off to a great start!

- ☐ Tobacco-free campus policy
- ☐ Healthy food and beverage options in vending machines and at gatherings
- ☐ Food preparation and storage facilities (for example, microwaves, refrigerators)
- ☐ On-site exercise facilities
- ☐ Planned workshops or print materials on health topics
- ☐ Employees trained in cardiopulmonary resuscitation (CPR) and automated external defibrillator (AED) use
- ☐ On-site vaccinations
- ☐ Insurance coverage for preventive services
- ☐ Paid time off for vacation, mental health, and sick days

What can you add or enhance to improve the wellness within your school community? Who will you assign to lead the initiative?

Wellness Initiative	Person Responsible	Implementation Date

Source: Adapted from National Association of Chronic Disease Directors. (2018). Healthy school, healthy staff, healthy students: A guide to improving school employee wellness. *Accessed at https://chronicdisease.org/resource/resmgr/school_health/school_employee_wellness/nacdd_schoolemployeewellness.pdf on October 17, 2022.*

CHAPTER 7

A Journey to Wellness

One day you will tell your story of how you overcame what you went through and it will be someone else's survival guide.

—Brené Brown

During one specific time in my life, I can say with vulnerable honesty that while I didn't use the bench in the bathroom at my workplace, I used the sofa in my boss's office. That was my bench. There were many mornings when I couldn't even collect myself, because in the mornings, everything would just hit me for whatever reason (perhaps because I'm a morning person and that's when my thinking is clearest).

Sometimes during that time, I would sit behind the wheel during my twenty-minute drive to work and sob. It would take me several minutes to pull myself together enough to even get out of the car and make it through the side door into my office. When I did make it through and was just about to close the door, I sometimes hoped no one would knock. Other times, I would take the extra few steps to my boss's office—my safe space—so I could pull it together and be present to work.

I went through that routine for a long time. Looking back, I can't imagine working in an environment where I didn't have a safe space. If I hadn't had a safe space, I would have taken a leave and been completely absent from work. The reason I was able to remain at work and give my best had everything to do with the environment I walked into every morning. In that environment, I was able to feel vulnerable enough to share with my boss what was happening in my life. I was working with team members who made me laugh. I was counting on my relationships with my colleagues; we could do things like go for a late lunch after the workday and be together for a couple of hours to genuinely enjoy ourselves. All those things were beneficial and valuable for me during that time.

In the context of an educational work environment, a *safe space* is a physical place or object, like a room, a sofa, or, yes, a bench in the bathroom. A *safe space* is also abstract: mental, emotional, social, and communal, and inherent in the culture (in the ways people behave toward one another on a day-to-day basis). This kind of safety can act as a vessel for survival, allowing people to continue to contribute even during difficult times.

To be clear, I don't think that experiencing personal difficulties means leaders should relax the standard for what and how an educator must contribute. During my difficulty, I understood I needed to show up physically and mentally and that my team, my colleagues, and our students depended on me. Leaders understand that some of the best, brightest, and most contributing people will have challenging times in life. In this chapter, I share how a real school, Paradise Charter Middle School (PCMS) in California, thrived amid a natural disaster that profoundly affected the entire community. In the aftermath of the most destructive wildfire in California's history, the leaders at PCMS utilized (as they had prior to the fire) strategies that share the leadership philosophies of the strategies I outline in this book. Employing these strategies looks different in different situations, in different schools, but all scenarios will be grounded in the principles of the trauma-compassionate approach and people-first leadership when the strategies are used effectively. Leaders can design an environment that creates a soft place for everyone to land. Educators deserve that, and students deserve it too. While the following real-world example is not meant to guide in a precise way, it is meant to inspire as you, too, employ the strategies of this book in a way that fits your unique situation and move beyond the bench to develop an education environment that provides a safe space—a culture of wellness—in which your colleagues and students may work and learn.

Working and Learning in Paradise

Paradise is located in Butte County, about eighty-five miles north of Sacramento and twelve miles east of Chico, nestled in the foothills of the Sierra Nevada in Northern California. PCMS serves about 150 students in grades 6 through 8, has a 21 percent minority matriculation, and economically disadvantaged students compose 43 percent of the population (U.S. News Education, n.d.). The school serves students and their families in a county where ACEs, drug abuse, and divorce-rate statistics are some of the highest in the state. Here's a quick numerical snapshot of Butte County, California.

- Has the third-highest divorce rate in the state (McKinley, Conger, Jolley, & Galarneau, 2021).
- Saw a 34 percent increase in overdose deaths between 2019 and 2020 (O'Brien, 2021).
- "Has notably higher childhood maltreatment rates than California overall, including neglect and abuse allegations" (Butte County Public Health, 2019–2022, p. 10).
- Has some of the highest ACEs scores in the state (Kidsdata, n.d.), including:

  76.5 percent of Butte County respondents reported one or more ACEs, which was considerably higher than the most recent data for statewide respondents (65.5%). . . . Further, Butte County respondents had higher rates than statewide respondents across all ACEs categories, with the most frequent being: substance use by a household member (37.8% vs. 26.1%); parental separation or divorce (37.3% vs. 26.7%); emotional or verbal abuse (35.2% vs. 34.9%); household member with mental illness (28.4% vs. 15.0%); and witnessing domestic violence (19.3% vs. 17.5%). (Butte County Public Health, 2019–2022, p. 10)

Much of these data were tied to the community for some time, while some of these grim numbers were exacerbated after the infamous Camp Fire swept through the county and town on November 8, 2018, leaving its already challenged residents devastated. This fire killed "85 people and destroyed nearly 19,000 homes, businesses, and other buildings" (Associated Press, 2021). It left most of the pre-fire population of approximately 27,000 people without homes, jobs, and everything they had once owned, and it left many without a path forward to build new homes (Siegler, 2019).

The traumas the people of Butte County experienced profoundly increased and continued to evolve after the fire. Despite these sobering statistics and an all-encompassing community tragedy, the students at PCMS excel academically and continue to do so. Based on data from the 2018–2019 and 2019–2020 school years, student test scores show 62 percent of students scored at or above the proficient level for mathematics, and 67 percent scored at or above for reading (U.S. News Education, n.d.). When compared to mathematics and reading proficiency scores across the state of California as a whole, the students scored 23 percent higher in mathematics and 20 percent higher in reading (U.S. News Education, n.d.). The school stands out as an example of a culture that allows the teachers, staff, and students to thrive and succeed in the face of trauma, stress, and even large-scale chaos. I knew a teacher at the school and heard many stories of the school's positive culture. This book provided the perfect opportunity for me to meet the principal (Chris Reid) and learn firsthand his approach to creating such a remarkable school culture. In this chapter, I share what I gleaned about Chris's leadership.

When I interviewed Chris (on the brink of his retirement), I also spoke with his incoming successor (Bev Landers) and a teacher (Brian Faith). At the end of the 2020–2021 school year, Chris had been principal for seventeen years. In my initial conversations with these three, I recognized (as I had suspected) that leadership played a pivotal role in curating the organizational culture at PCMS; leadership provided an environment where teachers feel safe, and leaders support and encourage staff to be creative in the interest of providing what's best for the students entrusted to them.

During our interview, Chris shared the core belief that guides his leadership style; he believes this belief is central to his success as a teacher and an educational leader. That belief, which derives from his strong commitment to his faith, is, to paraphrase, *Every student is the world's most important being.* That means students are no less important to Chris than the president, a Nobel Prize winner, or his own personal hero—or even when people compare students to other students who might be higher achieving, kinder, or more in need. No, Chris believes every single student is the most important.

While staff members had various individual ways of phrasing Chris's guiding value, they were unified in their belief in the importance of each student, and they agreed that to receive six hours a day to nurture and teach a student is a sacred trust parents and guardians grant to educators. This constant awareness and mindfulness of the sacred trust and unwavering support for his teachers threads through everything Chris said and did each day as the educational leader.

According to Brian, it is Chris's support and trust in his teachers that brings a sense of connection and community to the workplace. Brian has taught at PCMS since its inception in 1995, and he experienced the transformation from the first three or four years of unsettled leadership into the culture that Chris led.

Brian asserts:

> The culture is based on a simple kind of formula of just being really thoughtful about trying to take care of everybody, understanding that kids bring a backstory to school. And when they're misbehaving or whatever's going on with them, whatever their behaviors are at school, there's a reason for that. And it usually doesn't have anything to do with us. We understand that now.

> And I think it's important to understand that that's true about teachers too. Teachers are going through nasty divorces, their parents die, their kids are sick, and they're in car accidents, or they're having financial problems. We bring all that to the table too. So if administrators can understand that and ask more questions [when] you're not being yourself . . . and a teacher feels like they're trusted, they're more willing to share that stuff. So, to me, it's just that simple. It's not easy, but it's really simple—to just be mindful that people are in goofy spots. . . . I want people to understand that. It's not rocket science. It's just being there for each other. (B. Faith, personal communication, November 17, 2021)

Strategies for Cultural Wellness at Paradise

The shared belief in the importance of each student, educator, and staff member translates directly into what the leadership and staff at PCMS do every day in the classroom, at staff meetings, at parent-teacher conferences, and during disciplinary events for both students and staff. At the first staff meeting of his career, Chris recalled telling his teachers:

> We can never 'X out' students, period—no matter how much they [annoy] us, how exhausting they are, and no matter what their poor attitude is (and it can get really poor in middle school). And they're pretty smart, and they know how to push our buttons as adults. We can't X them out; they have a backstory, and we need to figure out how to support them really well. And then things are going to change. (C. Reid, personal communication, November 17, 2021)

To serve the students at his school, Chris understood his primary role: to serve the teachers of his school. The philosophy that no one is *X'ed out* (that is, dismissed or diminished) persisted in Chris's interactions with his staff and teachers. He took the strategies educators know are effective with the students and made them relevant to the adults in his care. By doing so, he enabled his teachers and staff to feel free to express themselves in their humanity. The following five sections describe how Chris amended those strategies and applied them to fit the needs of adult educators at PCMS, and particularly the needs of these educators while they were recovering from the stress of a natural disaster.

Adopt a Strengths-Based Approach

Twelve years into his thirty-seven-year career in education, the administration asked Chris to become a reading recovery specialist. He learned that instead of approaching first graders who have trouble reading from a deficit perspective (which means simply remediating deficits an assessment reveals), Chris learned to approach learning from a strengths-based model. This model required him to work from the known to the unknown, versus focusing on the unknown with no foundation. This was a profound paradigm shift for Chris, but he adopted this approach as a leader because he views his staff as his students. Always thoughtful and observant of his teachers, Chris identified their strengths and aimed to help them enhance those strengths, and then use those strengths to address their weaknesses. Chris said he recognized two things after learning and using this approach, (1) this is a slow process and (2) it works across the board with students and teachers. "I don't look at weaknesses. I look [for] the strengths of every human being. And I say, 'How can I work from that model from what's known and where they're strong and to get to the unknown?'" (C. Reid, personal communication, November 17, 2021).

Cultivate Passion

Chris premised his leadership approach on the notion that teachers are the experts in the classroom; they know their stuff. Thus, his primary mission was to find out how he could best support them in the classroom and on their professional journeys. One way Chris cultivated passion in his teachers was to structure teacher evaluations each year as an experience for self-reflection for each teacher instead of making them critical, evaluative, nerve-racking job appraisals. He wanted to know how his teachers desired to grow as educators, and how he could support them. Chris ensured his staff understood that working with him would be a journey of discovery together, in part, by getting to know them as people and reaching out to engage them professionally through things he learned they cared about. The following is an example of Chris engaging Brian by helping him incorporate his values and interests into his work. Brian recalls when Chris asked him to teach a vocal music class:

> Chris knows I'm a musician, and I've been a singer in bands forever. So a year or two before the fire, Chris came to me and said, "You should teach this vocal music class." I replied, "Look, I know how to sing. But I don't know how to teach how to sing." And Chris just worked on me for like, a year. And he says, "Just do it. Just do it. Just try it." So, I said I would try. It scared me to death.
>
> As it turned out, it was awesome because I had this phenomenal group of kids, talented kids. They're into it. They loved it. And we had this great little club of singers at various levels. And it was great. So, I went to him, and I said, "You know what I really need? I really need a keyboard because I need to be able to plunk out these melodies, so these kids can match these pitches." I told him, "I went to the Guitar Center, and they've got this keyboard that's 850 bucks, because I don't want some piece of junk." And he responds, "Buy

it." So, I came back with it the next day. A bit later, I went back to him, and I said, "You know, this tiny little PA [public address] system that I'm using isn't adequate. Kids can't hear themselves. I went to the Guitar Center, and there's this PA system, and it's 1,300 bucks. Maybe at the end of the year, we can talk about where money can come from for that." He responds, "Just buy it now. Just get it." So, I came back the next day with it. Those things have been transformational for that little program, and I think Chris knew that I needed to have some things in place, so I felt more comfortable teaching that class.

So, it's this culture where he understands what our strengths are, as well as the kinds of things we struggle with. He was blown away that I would be reticent to teach this class. I kept telling him that it was so important to me to do music well, that I didn't want to be a public failure at this thing, because I've never done that with music. And he sensed anything he could do to help would be beneficial. And he does that with all of us. And so I think that's a big part of what helps us feel comfortable . . . [allowing us to be] innovative and trying to do things that we know are going to help these kids buy into the thing that we're doing, which is education. (B. Faith, personal communication, November 17, 2021).

There's a lot to be said for connecting with your teachers and aligning them with what they're passionate about, even if what's inside your teachers' heads tells them they don't think they can. This relates directly to an element of servant leadership; that is, it "emphasizes the intrinsic value of each team member," which is also a commitment to the growth of others (Indeed Editorial Team, 2021). This specific story is significant in terms of creating a well culture because it set a powerful example of what this school values and how it connects community members beyond just a teacher and his vocal music students. From this course, talent began to emerge among the students and the teachers, and the space for sharing the human experience expanded. The school now hosts an annual talent show where "some insanely talented kids" perform not only vocally but also through dance and instrumental music (B. Faith, personal communication, November 17, 2021). Another teacher even started playing the drums in their Little Bulldog Blues Band.

Brian explained that his story, and so many others like it, was based in Chris's first priority of ensuring his teachers are there for the students because Chris realized that if the teachers don't like their jobs, then "the whole thing falls apart" (B. Faith, personal communication, November 17, 2021). You can attribute the school's student successes to autonomous decision making on behalf of the teachers, and Chris's willingness to invite teachers into a partnership which allowed them to act as thinking beings in discovering and implementing what is best for themselves and their students as they move through their professional development journey.

Acting as a substitute teacher and other acts championed Chris's vision of supporting teachers by caring for, honoring, appreciating, and emotionally supporting them daily. When a teacher needed to step away for a break, be home with a sick child, meet with Federal Emergency Management Agency (FEMA) representatives, or run an errand, Chris stepped in. The teachers benefited from knowing they had support available during their time of need.

Brian concluded that this kind of support, trust, and autonomy to succeed (and fail) builds confidence in teachers, and with that confidence, the teachers can be themselves. Students pick up on whether their teachers are comfortable in the classroom, with their subject material, and with being themselves, and this gives the students confidence. When teachers are comfortable, they can build important relationships with colleagues, students, and parents. The whole culture then just thrives.

Maintain Culture in the Face of Growth

When it came time to grow PCMS, Chris realized two things: (1) the school needed to grow because no one was leaving and everyone was moving up the pay scale, and (2) to maintain the culture, PCMS had to accomplish growth slowly while the school brought the right people into the fold.

PCMS could have grown overnight; it had a student waiting list that would immediately double the size of the school community. However, to maintain the special environment they'd so worked hard to build, the staff decided to grow over a period of four years. I realize this isn't an option for all schools, but it's not about PCMS being able to grow slowly, it's how the staff did it. It goes back to why teachers stay and includes infusing choice.

Chris collaborated with his teachers about how growth should happen, who would be a part of that growth, and how the teachers wanted it to look in terms of their own professional development. Two things stood out to me: (1) Chris honored his teachers by giving them a vision, and (2) he allowed the teachers to work together as a team to reach that vision.

The plan to grow slowly was in place before staff implemented the multiyear growth model. (Prior to this, the only occasion when the school needed to hire a teacher was when an English teacher went to be a missionary in Kenya.) However, because the school was not quite ready to implement the growth model, the administration hired Chris; he became an English teacher for a year until the school was ready to add students and teachers.

As the plan to grow began to form, Chris told his teachers, "I want you to drive." To explore further the teachers' desires and aspirations for their own professional journeys, he had them write out their dream schedules. He wanted to know how many prep periods, when those prep periods should be, and what classes they'd like to teach (or not teach). Chris then said to reach this vision, they would work as a team. Next, they added one additional sixth-grade class each year for three years.

Changes for the better emerged from the team's hard work to accommodate their dream schedules. Chris identified a mathematics teacher whom he felt did not belong in the mathematics classroom (even though his credential allowed him to teach it). And another teacher said he was tired of teaching physical education. By the end of three years, the community had made significant shifts and all the teachers who had submitted a dream schedule were now teaching those schedules. Teachers were more aligned with their passions through their own choices. Teachers were motivated and accountable! Chris concluded by adding he believed the teachers owned the school as much as he did, and this was a powerful experience for them. (C. Reid, personal communication, November 17, 2021).

Hire Into a Culture of Wellness

When creating a culture of wellness, I've talked about how it's important to work with existing teachers on your team and in your organization to ensure they meet their fullest potential in their journey by supporting them, realigning them when needed, and letting them go to their next roles when the fit isn't right. Letting someone go is difficult in nearly any case. Prior to the first teacher dismissal I ever had to administer, my superintendent met with me beforehand. He looked at me and said, "Would you want that person teaching your child?" While I didn't have children at the time, it was still the ultimate clarifying question. While most, maybe all, people who are in education are what Chris called "incredibly golden people," the superintendent and I agreed that some people do not have the necessary skills for the day-to-day grind in the classroom (C. Reid, personal communication, November 17, 2021). If people can't develop those skills in a reasonable time frame, leaders must honor the teachers and students by letting them go.

To avoid the likelihood of having to let a teacher go, leaders can hire for zeal, as I discussed in chapter 6 (page 95). The unique nature of the hiring process that Chris and his team created is an excellent example of hiring with the aim to build and maintain a culture of wellness.

When Chris told me he established a hiring committee that included parents, board members, and staff, he laughed and said everyone wanted to be on the committee because everyone was so invested (C. Reid, personal communication,

November 17, 2021). Ultimately, Chris and his teachers decided eight was a manageable number. Next, the eight-member committee spent time dreaming together to build a vision for each job opening: Who might this person be? Through that collective envisioning, the committee articulated what each role truly needed. They asked themselves, "In addition to credential, what is this person's demeanor? Is he or she engaging? Collaborative? A strong communicator and listener? Does this person express empathy and patience? Is he or she a lifelong learner? Can parents entrust their children to this person?" The committee agreed they would not hire unless the person was an absolute superstar. Chris told me the committee also decided they would "steal" somebody who was thriving somewhere else (C. Reid, personal communication, November 17, 2021). Chris admitted this is the best hiring practice; find someone who is already thriving, even in a completely different position than what they are hiring for. He provided the following example.

There was a gentleman who was, Chris said, one of the finest administrators he ever served under. Chris continued, "This administrator's history was as a high school counselor. He knew nothing about middle school. But he was a dynamic, thriving human being, who understood human relationships, and understood how to support educators. He was a marvel. He was thriving" (C. Reid, personal communication, November 17, 2021). So the PCMS hiring committee hired this counselor and one other, and the school is fortunate to still have them there today. The committee held out for their two superstars.

I heard it said once that when you leave a job, make sure it's not because you're running from something, but running to something else. You don't need to hold individuals running to your school accountable every day in the traditional sense because when they come to you, they seek growth and further professional development. They are not leaving something unhappy and looking elsewhere for a solution to their unhappiness. They are already passionate, enthusiastic, and successful, and they are walking into what is already exciting for them.

Maintain and Replicate a Culture of Wellness

When you've got something good going, naturally, you want to grow it and include as many students and families as you can, right? The Paradise community recognized their little middle school was a special place. In fact, Chris shared with me that other teachers, principals, superintendents, bus drivers, and special education teachers would send their children to the school (C. Reid, personal communication, November 17, 2021). And some did it at great professional cost. When those who lead, work, and teach elsewhere send their children to your school, it divulges the impact of a school's environment. Chris said this message is very powerful for his teachers and staff.

In the years since the fire, Chris and his staff have felt pressure from parents in the community to grow the school and even open a high school. Many ask, "Why can't you replicate it? Why can't you just keep growing?" Admittedly, one of the reasons for their success is this school has maintained a fairly small size, even though it grew by 50 percent. What do you do when your organization is not so small? Or it's not a middle school?

While you may not necessarily be in a small school, you can create a small-school environment by keeping teams and departments at manageable numbers for supervision. It's called *span of control* and refers to the number of direct reports a manager or supervisor has (SHRM, n.d.). "It is also a management principle used when determining how many direct reports a manager can have and still be able to manage effectively" (SHRM, n.d.). This number varies with the type of industry, the work leaders and supervisors perform, and their direct reports. For example, I have worked in a larger school system where the principals did not report to the district superintendent but rather chief area officers. This made the executive leadership more accessible at the local level.

There's always the argument that an organization is top-heavy with administrators, spending more money on leadership and not enough on teachers. But there are creative ways to structure your organization so no one works in a silo and others are not overwhelmed and ineffectively leading too many at once. It's incumbent on the leader to ensure both that the span of control is appropriate and that everyone is communicating. For example, Why can't you have an instructional leader who works a partial day as a teacher but who also leads a small team of people? Budgets, classroom sizes, and so on are all concerns, but as a leader, you must be prepared to think creatively when addressing these issues. Leaders are the people tasked with finding ways around concerns in the interest of what's best for teachers and students. The roadblocks you encounter can work in your favor when you separate your vision from the culture that currently exists, looking beyond those roadblocks to the culture that *can* exist.

As we grow at the iCan Dream Center, one of the things we definitely want is to maintain a small-school environment no matter how large we get. But one of the things I now realize is that having a new, smaller nucleus of team members makes all the difference in the world. I think it's imperative that leaders have a finger on the pulse of their teams.

I asked Chris if he thought what he and his team created at PCMS is replicable in any educational organization. He said the state of California recognized that public educators wanted to be creative, to be able to better meet the needs of students in their district, and added, "I think it's replicable" (C. Reid, personal communication, November 17, 2021). He explained it's the core values the leader lives by daily that contribute to the culture. It's the authentic leader who sees him, her-, or themself as a servant and transformational leader. It's the leader who understands that it's the teachers who are the ones with the power. It's the leader who recognizes teachers need support daily. It's the leader who aspires to set up situations where teachers can build relationships and empower them to hang out and connect as human beings, and get to know others' backstories better. It's the leader who frees up the teacher by taking away some of the work the teacher doesn't need to be doing. It's the leader who will trust that teachers know what's best for the students in their classroom and how to best serve them.

It comes down to how you use the tools you have, and how creative you can get by inventing new ones that fit your organization. It doesn't matter what school you come from. It can be a small religious school, a large public school, a charter school, a daycare; it doesn't matter. Regardless of what environment you find yourself in, change is always an option. You can get worse, you can stay the same, or you can get better. It's a choice.

Although this chapter highlights one school and what that school is doing to be successful and to build and maintain a culture of wellness—a culture where students and teachers grow and thrive—know that there are educational leaders finding success with these methods every day around the world.

It took the PCMS seventeen years to get where it is today. It's a slow, methodical process to change an organization's culture, and it starts with you, the leader. Don't rush it. Start by making one small choice and taking one intentional step in the direction of what's better.

Please use The Culture Within section to further explore the contents of this chapter through the lens of your own experiences, values, and perceptions.

The Culture Within

How does your organization compare to PCMS? What is similar, what is different, and what drives these similarities and differences?

What modifications might you make to any of the strategies Chris uses in this chapter to best fit your organization?

In what ways do you feel you are connected to a bigger purpose in your role? How would you like to be remembered or regarded at retirement? Reflect on what you need to do to move in the direction of your desired trajectory.

Epilogue

> Almost everything will work again if you unplug it for a few minutes, including you.
>
> —Anne Lamott

I accumulated more than thirty days of absence during my freshman year of high school. No, I was not school avoidant. I was not ill. And I was not ditching school to participate in nefarious activities. You may find it surprising that in these absences, I had the full support of my mother.

For context, the summer prior to ninth grade, both my father and grandfather succumbed to their battles with illness. Amid the pain of becoming a widow and losing her father, my mother was cognizant of the need to recharge. Occasionally, she would say, "It's a good day for a mental health day," or she would plan an outing or vacation during the school week. To be clear (grief aside), the standard for my school performance was unwavering. I was never permitted to earn less than a B+, so my mother looked for my feedback on the timing of these breaks. I share this to say that my mother was the first to teach me about self-care and the need to recharge. I completed high school in three years, earning my diploma and a full academic scholarship at age sixteen.

I was able to excel academically (and, later, professionally) because I learned early to attend to my emotional needs to create optimal performance conditions. My mother's parenting style has always been progressive. While the term *self-care* was not common in the '90s, my mother instinctively responded to my needs, and by doing so, created neuropathways in my brain that reinforced the importance of self-care. My mother also inspired me to be a leader who actively cultivates work and learning environments that value self-care.

Source: © 2019 by Neesha Stringfellow. Used with permission.

Figure E.1: The author and her mother.

A few words about the nature of self-care. Self-care is not self-indulgent. Self-care is not a reward for a sacrifice you make. *Self-care* is a habit you create and maintain for physical, emotional, and mental well-being. It's giving yourself permission to pause regularly (a must-do to be an effective leader), because pausing allows you to maintain adequate energy to give to those you lead. If you constantly give of yourself without renewing your strength, you will eventually give yourself and everything you have away. When you are burned out, you cannot effectively lead. Self-care is necessary if you wish to create an environment where students and teachers both achieve what they are capable of and deserve.

I am grateful that my mother modeled self-care for me. In the same way, those you serve are taking note of your words and actions. When you engage in self-care practices, you are not only ensuring your own wellness but also modeling wellness for those you lead.

Modeling Self-Care as a Critical Action in Leading a Physically, Emotionally, and Socially Safe School Culture

Late one night, I sat at my computer pounding out an email to an employee for the following day. Suddenly, it struck me cold: *I wasn't modeling self-care*. In fact, I was setting a terrible example. I looked at the time on my computer: ten minutes to midnight. My employee would see the time stamp on my email. By sending that email, I thought the following.

- I am not modeling wellness.
- I am not adhering to the work-life boundaries I set up for myself.
- I am deviating from my values.
- I am not setting a good example.
- I am definitely not cultivating an environment that feels safe.

So I stopped writing that email and went to bed.

To honor the well-being of those you lead, it's essential that you value yourself and practice self-care. If you are burned out, you serve no one at all. A culture of wellness starts with a leader devoted to wellness in mind, body, and soul. Self-care is critical to a physically, emotionally, and socially safe school culture.

When leaders engage in self-care and allow employees to do so, they move beyond the bathroom bench as their only place of refuge into a culture that already functions as a safe, comfortable place for all.

So how do you serve the people in your organization without sacrificing yourself? To show up as an effective leader in your organization, lead by example and inspire.

References and Resources

Ainomugisha, G. (n.d.). *7 concerning signs of a toxic work culture.* Accessed at https://inside.6q.io/toxic-work-culture on October 17, 2022.

Allarakha, S. (2021, February 8). *What are the 3 types of trauma?* Accessed at https://medicinenet.com/what_are_the_3_types_of_trauma/article.htm on October 17, 2022.

American Federation of Teachers. (2017). *2017 educator quality of work life survey.* Accessed at https://aft.org/sites/default/files/media/2017/2017_eqwl_survey_web.pdf on October 17, 2022.

American Psychiatric Association. (1987). *Diagnostic and statistical manual of mental disorders: DSM-III-R* (3rd ed., rev.). Washington, DC: Author.

American Psychological Association. (2018, June 27). *Vacation time recharges US workers, but positive effects vanish within days, new survey finds* [Press release]. Accessed at https://apa.org/news/press/releases/2018/06/vacation-recharges-workers on October 17, 2022.

Associated Press. (2021, November 9). "We will never forget": California marks 3rd anniversary of deadly wildfire that leveled Paradise. *Record Searchlight.* Accessed at https://redding.com/story/news/local/fires/2021/11/09/california-fires-camp-fire-3-years-later-wildfire-cleanup-california-wildfires-paradise/6356476001 on October 17, 2022.

Atik, S., & Çelik, O. T. (2020). An investigation of the relationship between school principals' empowering leadership style and teachers' job satisfaction: The role of trust and psychological empowerment. *International Online Journal of Educational Sciences, 12*(3), 177–193.

Barbuto, J. E., Jr. (2007, October). *Becoming a servant leader: Do you have what it takes?* Accessed at https://extensionpublications.unl.edu/assets/html/g1481/build/g1481.htm on January 2, 2022.

Beck, J. L., & Servage, L. (2018) *"Who will help me to do well?" How to best support the professional growth of Alberta's newest teachers.* Edmonton, Alberta, Canada: Alberta Teachers' Association. Accessed at https://legacy.teachers.ab.ca/SiteCollectionDocuments/ATA/Publications/Research/COOR-101-17%20How%20to%20Support%20Alberta%27s%20Newest%20Teachers.pdf on January 19, 2023.

Bence, S. (2021, December 17). *The difference between acute and chronic trauma*. Accessed at https://verywellhealth.com/acute-trauma-vs-chronic-trauma-5208875 on October 17, 2022.

Benjet, C., Bromet, E., Karam, E. G., Kessler, R. C., McLaughlin, K. A., Ruscio, A. M.,et al. (2016). *The epidemiology of traumatic event exposure worldwide: Results from the World Mental Health Survey Consortium* . Accessed at https://pubmed.ncbi.nlm.nih.gov/26511595 on February 21, 2022.

Best Accredited Colleges. (2021, October 20). *Top 5 reasons why public schools are failing our children*. Accessed at https://bestaccreditedcolleges.org/articles/top-5-reasons-why-public-schools-are-failing-our-children.html on October 17, 2022.

Blanchard, K. (n.d.). *Servant leadership for a next generation workforce*. Accessed at https://kenblanchard.com/Solutions/Servant-Leadership-Essentials on January 2, 2023.

Brown, B. (2018, October 15). *Clear is kind. Unclear is unkind*. Accessed at https://brenebrown.com/articles/2018/10/15/clear-is-kind-unclear-is-unkind on October 17, 2022.

Brown, D. (2016). *Childhood trauma: America's hidden health crisis* [Video file]. Accessed at https://acesconnection.com/g/los-angeles-aces-connection/clip/childhood-trauma-america-s-hidden-health-crisis on January 19, 2023.

Buckle, J. (n.d.). *21 quick questions to check in on your students' well-being in 2022–23* [Blog post]. Accessed at https://panoramaed.com/blog/21-questions-check-in-student-sel-wellbeing#:~:text=Bi%2Dweekly%20or%20monthly%20student,especially%20in%20a%20virtual%20environment on January 19, 2023.

Burch, J. (2019, March 29). *Why you should start your class with behavior check-ins* [Blog post]. Accessed at https://blog.esc13.net/why-you-should-start-your-class-with-behavior-check-ins on October 17, 2022.

Burnout. (n.d.). In *Merriam-Webster's online dictionary*. Accessed at https://merriam-webster.com/dictionary/burnout on February 21, 2022.

Burns, J. M. (1978). *Leadership*. New York: Harper & Row.

Butte County Public Health. (2019–2022). *Community health assessment: Executive summary*. Accessed at www.buttecounty.net/Portals/21/Admin/Accreditation/Public/CHA2019_ExecutiveSummary.pdf?ver=2019–11–05–151527–793 on February 25, 2022.

Cafasso, J. (2021, April 14). *Traumatic events*. Accessed at https://healthline.com/health/traumatic-events on October 4, 2021.

Camp Fire (2018). (2023, January 18). In *Wikipedia*. Accessed at https://en.wikipedia.org/wiki/Camp_Fire_(2018) on January 23, 2023.

Castrillion, C. (2021, May 23). *Why taking vacation time could save your life*. Accessed at https://forbes.com/sites/carolinecastrillon/2021/05/23/why-taking-vacation-time-could-save-your-life/?sh=6ab7294724de on October 17, 2022.

Center on the Developing Child. (2015, March 19). *Key concepts: Toxic stress*. Accessed at https://developingchild.harvard.edu/science/key-concepts/toxic-stress on March 21, 2022.

Centers for Disease Control and Prevention. (2019, November 5). *Adverse childhood experiences (ACEs): Preventing early trauma to improve adult health*. Accessed at https://cdc.gov/vitalsigns/aces on February 22, 2022.

Centers for Disease Control and Prevention. (2020, September 17). *Infographic: 6 guiding principles to a trauma-informed approach.* Accessed at https://cdc.gov/cpr/infographics/6_principles_trauma_info.htm on October 17, 2022.

Centers for Disease Control and Prevention. (2022, April 6). *Fast facts: Preventing adverse childhood experiences.* Accessed at https://cdc.gov/violenceprevention/aces/fastfact.html on February 22, 2022.

Chen, G. (2020, September 3). *Why 82% of public schools are failing* [Blog post]. Accessed at https://publicschoolreview.com/blog/why-82-of-public-schools-are-failing on October 17, 2022.

Clutch. (2018, May 9). *Nearly half of office workers value community in the workplace.* Accessed at https://prnewswire.com/news-releases/nearly-half-of-office-workers-value-community-in-the-workplace-682214991.html on May 4, 2022.

CNN. (2018, July 30). *The endangered starry sky.* Accessed at https://youtube.com/watch?v=VxZtwXjEHkE on July 3, 2021.

Compassion. (n.d.). In *Merriam-Webster's online dictionary.* Accessed at https://merriam-webster.com/dictionary/compassion on May 1, 2022.

Conzemius, A. E., & O'Neill, J. (2014). *The handbook for SMART school teams: Revitalizing best practices for collaboration* (2nd ed.). Bloomington, IN: Solution Tree Press.

Covey, S. R. (1989). *The seven habits of highly effective people: Restoring the character ethic.* New York: Free Press.

Curi, M. (2018, June 15). *A short history of trauma-informed care.* Accessed at https://iowawatch.org/2018/06/15/a-short-history-of-trauma-informed-care/ on February 18, 2023.

Dallmann-Jones, A. (2019, August 3). *8 characteristics of a functional family.* Accessed at https://doctorzest.com/family/8-characteristics-of-a-functional-family on October 17, 2022.

Deal, T. E., & Peterson, K. D. (2016). *Shaping school culture: Pitfalls, paradoxes, and promises* (3rd ed.). San Francisco: Jossey-Bass.

De La Rosa, S. (2020, July 10). *Study: More than half of students lost 39% of year's learning over summer.* Accessed at https://k12dive.com/news/study-more-than-half-of-students-lost-39-of-years-learning-over-summer/581365 on October 17, 2022.

Donald, J. N., Atkins, P. W. B., Parker, P. D., Christie, A. M., & Ryan, R. M. (2016, December). Daily stress and the benefits of mindfulness: Examining the daily and longitudinal relations between present-moment awareness and stress responses. *Journal of Research in Personality, 65,* 30–37.

Drexler, K. A., Quist-Nelson, J., & Weil, A. B. (2022). Intimate partner violence and trauma-informed care in pregnancy. *American Journal of Obstetrics & Gynecology* MFM, *4*(2).

Duquesne University School of Nursing. (2020, October 26). *What are the 6 principles of trauma-informed care?* [Blog Post]. Accessed at https://onlinenursing.duq.edu/blog/what-are-the-6-principles-of-trauma-informed-care on January 25, 2023.

Engebretson, J. (2016, June 16). *Self-care: Putting your oxygen mask on first* [Slideshow]. Accessed at https://nihb.org/docs/06162016/Self%20Care%20Putting%20Your%20Oxygen%20Mask%20on%20First.pdf on January 25, 2023.

Erlenbusch, B., & Factor, D. (2019, November 20). *Opinion: All doctors should practice trauma-informed care.* Accessed at https://calhealthreport.org/2019/11/20/opinion-all-doctors-should-practice-trauma-informed-care on October 18, 2022.

Eustress. (n.d.). In *Cambridge Dictionary online.* Accessed at https://dictionary.cambridge.org/us/dictionary/english/eustress on December 30, 2022.

Felitti, V. J., Anda, R. F., Nordenberg, D., Williamson, D. F., Spitz, A. M., Edwards, V., et al. (1998). Relationship of childhood abuse and household dysfunction to many of the leading causes of death in adults—The adverse childhood experiences (ACE) study. *American Journal of Preventive Medicine, 14*(4), 245–258.

Frederique, N. (2020, November 13). *What do the data reveal about violence in schools?* Accessed at https://nij.ojp.gov/topics/articles/what-do-data-reveal-about-violence-schools on October 18, 2022.

Friedman, M. J. (n.d.) *PTSD history and overview.* Accessed at https://www.ptsd.va.gov/professional/treat/essentials/history_ptsd.asp on February 9, 2022.

Frothingham, M. B. (2021, October 6). *Fight, flight, freeze, or fawn: What this response means.* Accessed at https://simplypsychology.org/fight-flight-freeze-fawn.html on December 30, 2022.

Gaines, P., & Pratt-Kielley, E. (2019, October 11). *California's first surgeon general: Screen every student for childhood trauma.* Accessed at https://nbcnews.com/news/nbcblk/california-s-first-surgeon-general-screen-every-student-childhood-trauma-n1064286 on October 4, 2021.

Georgsdottir, M. T., Sigurdardottir, S., & Gunnthorsdottir, H. (2021). "This is the result of something else": Experiences of men that abused drugs and had experienced childhood trauma. *American Journal of Men's Health, 15*(2).

Giurge, L. M., & Woolley, K. (2020, July 22). Don't work on vacation. Seriously. *Harvard Business Review.* Accessed at https://hbr.org/2020/07/dont-work-on-vacation-seriously on October 18, 2022.

GoodTherapy.org Team. (2016, July 14). *Vicarious trauma* [Blog post]. Accessed at https://www.goodtherapy.org/blog/psychpedia/vicarious-trauma on February 25, 2022.

Greater Good Magazine. (n.d.). *What is compassion?* Accessed at https://greatergood.berkeley.edu/topic/compassion/definition on October 21, 2021.

Greenleaf, R. K. (1970). *The servant as leader.* Boston: The Center for Servant Leadership.

Greenleaf, R. K. (1998). *The power of servant leadership: Essays.* San Francisco: Berrett-Koehler.

Gunn, T. M., & McRae, P. A. (2021). Better understanding the professional and personal factors that influence beginning teacher retention in one Canadian province. *International Journal of Educational Research Open, 2*,.Accessed at https://www.sciencedirect.com/science/article/pii/S2666374021000431 on April 3, 2023.

Hammond, Z. (2015). *Culturally responsive teaching and the brain: Promoting authentic engagement and rigor among culturally and linguistically diverse students.* Thousand Oaks, CA: Corwin.

Hancock, L., & Bryant, R. A. (2018, September 27). Perceived control and avoidance in posttraumatic stress. *European Journal of Psychotraumatology, 9*(1). Accessed at https://www.ncbi.nlm.nih.gov/pmc/articles/PMC6161595 on October 18, 2022.

Harris, N. B. (2014, September). *How childhood trauma affects health across a lifetime* [Video file]. TEDEd 2014. Accessed at https://ed.ted.com/lessons/eczPoVp6 on January 19, 2023.

Harvard Graduate School of Education. (2023). *Providing wait-time for students to process and gain confidence.* Accessed at https://instructionalmoves.gse.harvard.edu/providing-wait-time-students-process-and-gain-confidence on May 4, 2022.

Health Care Toolbox. (n.d). *What is culturally-sensitive trauma-informed care?* Accessed at https://healthcaretoolbox.org/culturally-sensitive-trauma-informed-care on March 2, 2022.

Hearing. (n.d.). In *Merriam-Webster's online dictionary.* Accessed at https://merriam-webster.com/dictionary/hearing on September 20, 2022.

Hemati, A., & Moradi, S. (2021). Job burnout in public and special school teachers. *Clinical Psychology and Special Education, 10*(2), 63–75.

Herman, K., Hickmon-Rosa, J., & Reinke, W. M. (2018). Empirically derived profiles of teacher stress, burnout, self-efficacy, and copying associated with student outcomes. *Journal of Positive Behavior Interventions, 20*(2), 90–100. Accessed at https://researchgate.net/publication/320262480_Empirically_Derived_Profiles_of_Teacher_Stress_Burnout_Self-Efficacy_and_Coping_and_Associated_Student_Outcomes on October 18, 2022.

The Human Condition Editorial Team. (2021, October 30). *Adverse childhood experiences (ACEs): Impact, prevention, and treatment.* Accessed at https://thehumancondition.com/adverse-childhood-experiences on October 18, 2022.

IES. (n.d.). Check and connect. *What Works Clearinghouse.* Accessed at https://ies.ed.gov/ncee/wwc/EvidenceSnapshot/78 on February 20, 2023.

Indeed Editorial Team. (2021, March 15). *10 principles of servant leadership.* Accessed at https://www.indeed.com/career-advice/career-development/servant-leader-principles on October 28, 2021.

Informed. (n.d.). In *Merriam-Webster's online dictionary.* Accessed at https://merriam-webster.com/dictionary/informed on October 21, 2021.

Jamieson, K. (2019, March 26). *Toxic stress and ACEs.* Accessed at https://centerforchildcounseling.org/toxic-stress-and-aces on January 2, 2023.

Kaprál, J. (2018, September 10). These 7 companies encourage sleeping on the job. But why? [Blog post]. Kickresume Blog. Accessed at https://blog.kickresume.com/these-7-companies-encourage-sleeping-on-the-job-but-why/ on April 12, 2023.

Kenzie Academy from Southern New Hampshire University. (2020, June 18). *Why community matters in the workplace* [Blog post]. Accessed at https://kenzie.snhu.edu/blog/why-community-matters-in-the-workplace on May 4, 2022.{add entry]

Khan, H., Rehmat, M., Butt, T. H., Farooqi, S., & Asim, J. (2020). Impact of transformational leadership on work performance, burnout and social loafing: A mediation model. *Future Business Journal, 6*(1), 1–13.

Kidsdata. (n.d.). *Prevalence of adverse childhood experiences (adult retrospective; CA only)*. Accessed at https://kidsdata.org/topic/1969/aces-brfss/table#fmt=2486&loc=2&tf=153&ch=89,90,1273,1256,1274,1259 on February 25, 2022.

Korejan, M. M., & Shahbazi, H. (2016). An analysis of the transformational leadership theory. *Journal of Fundamental and Applied Sciences, 8*(3S), 452–461.

Lai, F.-Y., Tang, H.-C., Lu, S.-C., Lee, Y.-C., & Lin, C.-C. T. (2020). Transformational leadership and job performance: The mediating role of work engagement. *SAGE Open, 10*(1). https://doi.org/10.1177/2158244019899085

Lamoreux, K. (2021, June 11). *How stress can be a good thing*. Accessed at https://psychcentral.com/stress/is-stress-good-for-you on October 18, 2022.

Laub, J. (n.d.). *Servant leader discipline #3: Builds community*. Accessed at https://servantleaderperformance.com/servant-leader-discipline-3-builds-community on January 2, 2023.

Leading Effectively Staff. (2022, November 24). *The core leadership skills you need in every role*. Accessed at https://ccl.org/articles/leading-effectively-articles/fundamental-4-core-leadership-skills-for-every-career-stage on January 2, 2023.

Lebow, H. I. (2021, July 2). *What is complex trauma and how does it develop?* Accessed at https://psychcentral.com/ptsd/complex-trauma-a-step-by-step-description-of-how-it-develops on October 18, 2022.

Lehigh University. (2016, July 27). *After-hours email expectations negatively impact employee well-being*. Accessed at https://sciencedaily.com/releases/2016/07/160727110906.htm on October 18, 2022.

Lencioni, P. M. (2016). *The ideal team player: How to recognize and cultivate the three essential virtues—A leadership fable*. Hoboken, NJ: Wiley.

Levine, P. A. (1997). *Waking the tiger: Healing trauma—The innate capacity to transform overwhelming experiences*. Berkeley, CA: North Atlantic Books.

Lewis, M. (2016, April 4). *Why we're hardwired to hate uncertainty*. Accessed at https://theguardian.com/commentisfree/2016/apr/04/uncertainty-stressful-research-neuroscience on October 18, 2022.

Listening. (n.d.). In *Merriam-Webster's online dictionary*. Accessed at https://merriam-webster.com/dictionary/listening on October 28, 2021.

Loewus, L. (2021, May 4). Why teachers leave—or don't: A look at the numbers. *Education Week*. Accessed at https://edweek.org/teaching-learning/why-teachers-leave-or-dont-a-look-at-the-numbers/2021/05 on October 18, 2022.

MacNeil, A. J., Prater, D. L., & Busch, S. (2009). The effects of school culture and climate on student achievement. *International Journal of Leadership in Education, 12*(1), 73–84. Accessed at https://tandfonline.com/doi/full/10.1080/13603120701576241 on March 11, 2022.

Marco Learning. (2020, April 13). *The rise of teacher stress*. Accessed at https://marcolearning.com/crayons-and-cortisol-the-epidemic-of-teacher-stress/#:~:text=From%20an%20outside%20perspective%2C%20teaching,stressful%20occupation%20in%20America%20today on June 23, 2022.

McKinley, Conger, Jolley, & Galarneau, LLP. (2021, May 28). *These counties have the highest divorce rates in California* [Blog post]. Accessed at https://mcjglaw.com/blog/these-counties-have-the-highest-divorce-rates-in-california on January 19, 2023.

Mcleod, S. (2022, April 4). Maslow's hierarchy of needs. *Simply Psychology*. Accessed at https://simplypsychology.org/maslow.html on October 18, 2022.

Meador, D. (2019, July 1). *Basic strategies for providing support in the classroom*. Accessed at https://thoughtco.com/strategies-for-structure-in-the-classroom-4169394#:~:text=A%20structured%20classroom%20often%20translates,freedoms%20that%20they%20can%20abuse on October 18, 2022.

Melgar, L. (2019, May 17). *Are school shootings becoming more frequent? We ran the numbers.* Accessed at https://gunsandamerica.org/story/19/05/17/are-school-shootings-becoming-more-frequent-we-ran-the-numbers on October 18, 2022.

Miller, G. E. (2023, January 10.). *The U.S. is the most overworked developed nation in the world.* Accessed at https://20somethingfinance.com/american-hours-worked-productivity-vacation on January 30, 2023.

Muhammad, A. (2018). *Transforming school culture: How to overcome staff division* (2nd ed.). Bloomington, IN: Solution Tree Press.

National Association of Chronic Disease Directors. (2018). *Healthy school, healthy staff, healthy students: A guide to improving school employee wellness*. Accessed at https://chronicdisease.org/resource/resmgr/school_health/school_employee_wellness/nacdd_schoolemployeewellness.pdf on October 17, 2022.

National Center for PTSD. (2021, September 10) *How common is PTSD in adults?* Accessed at https://ptsd.va.gov/understand/common/common_adults.asp on February 20, 2022.

National Child Traumatic Stress Network. (n.d.). *Complex trauma*. Accessed at https://nctsn.org/what-is-child-trauma/trauma-types/complex-trauma#:~:text=Complex%20trauma%20describes%20both%20children%27s,as%20abus on February 15, 2022.

National Education Association. (2018). *NEA's school crisis guide: Help and healing in a time of crisis*. Washington, DC: Author. Accessed at https://www.nea.org/sites/default/files/2020-07/NEA%20School%20Crisis%20Guide%202018.pdf on January 26, 2023.

New Perspectives. (n.d.). *The history of psychological trauma*. Accessed at https://newperspectivesinc.com/the-history-of-psychological-trauma on February 22, 2022.

Niroga Institute. (2021, June 20). *What is teacher burnout?* [Video file]. Accessed at https://youtube.com/watch?v=_Nw14J61BVQ on January 25, 2023.

O'Brien, M. (2021, July 21). *Drug overdose deaths in Butte County* [Press release]. Butte Interagency Narcotics Task Force. Accessed at https://www.buttecounty.net/Portals/30/Press%20Releases/20210722_OD.doc?ver=2021-07-22-153554-270 on January 23, 2023.

Paradise. (n.d.). In *Oxford Learner's Dictionaries online*. Accessed at https://oxfordlearnersdictionaries.com/us/definition/english/paradise?q=Paradise on September 14, 2022.

Pennsylvania State University. (2016, September). *Teacher stress and health: Effects on teachers, students, and schools* [Issue brief]. Accessed at https://prevention.psu.edu/uploads/files/rwjf430428-TeacherStress.pdf on October 18, 2022.

Peterson, K. D. (1998, November). Toxic cultures and the problems of change. *Reform Talk, 11*. Accessed at http://archive.wceruw.org/ccvi/pub/ReformTalk/Year_1998/Nov_98_Reform _Talk_11.html on October 18, 2022.

Peterson, K. D. (2002, Summer). Positive or negative. *Journal of Staff Development*. Accessed at https://www.nesacenter.org/uploaded/conferences/FLC/2014/handouts /Kent_Peterson/KP_JSD_Pos_Neg_Cult_copy.pdf on March 21, 2022.

Razzetti, G. (2018, September 19). *How to overcome the fear of change: Become the author of your own life* [Blog post]. Accessed at https://fearlessculture.design/blog-posts/how-to-overcome -the-fear-of-change on January 3, 2023.

Relias. (n.d.). *Addressing trauma: 5 key elements to trauma-informed care* [White paper]. Accessed at https://relias.com/resource/5-key-elements-to-trauma-informed-care?aliId=0 on June 25, 2021.

Rimbey, C. (2021). *School violence: Definition, history, causes & effects* [Video file]. Accessed at https://study.com/academy/lesson/school-violence-definition-history-causes-effects.html on January 23, 2023.

Ryan, R. M., & Deci, E. L. (2000). Intrinsic and extrinsic motivations: Classic definitions and new directions. *Contemporary Educational Psychology, 25*(1), 54–67.

Saam, K., & Matthey, R. (2021, May 12). Paradise is the fastest growing city in California, according to new data. . Accessed at https://krcrtv.com/news /local/paradise-is-the-fastest-growing-city-in-california on October 18, 2022.

Sage, F. (n.d.). *The man on the subway: From* The seven habits of highly effective people *by Steven* [sic] *Covey*. Accessed at https://florasage.com/the-man-on-the-subway on October 17, 2022.

Schein, E. H. (1985). *Organizational culture and leadership*. San Francisco: Jossey-Bass.

Seppälä, E. (2017, August 17). *Three science-based reasons vacations boost productivity* [Blog post]. Accessed at https://psychologytoday.com/us/blog/feeling-it/201708/three-science -based-reasons-vacations-boost-productivity on October 18, 2022.

Shoff, D. (2020, February 27). *Servant leader principle #8—Stewardship*. Accessed at https://leader-as-servant.com/2020/02/27/servant-leader-principle-8-stewardship on January 2, 2022.

Siegler, K. (2019, May 8). *More than 1,000 families still searching for homes 6 months after the camp fire*. NPR. Accessed at https://www.npr.org/2019/05/08/721057281/more-than-1-000- families-still-searching-for-homes-6-months -after-the-camp-fire on February 16, 2023.

Society for Human Resource Management. (n.d.). *Span of control*. Accessed at https://shrm .org/resourcesandtools/tools-and-samples/hr-glossary/pages/span-of-control.aspx on April 21, 2022.

Society for Human Resource Management. (2016, February 23). *Defining organizational culture*. Accessed at https://shrm.org/resourcesandtools/hr-topics/behavioral-competencies /global-and-cultural-effectiveness/pages/defining-culture.aspx on December 21, 2021.

Spacey, J. (2018, December 15). *47 examples of the human experience.* Accessed at https://simplicable.com/new/human-experience on October 18, 2022.

Spears, L. C. (2010). *Character and servant leadership: Ten characteristics of effective, caring leaders.* Accessed at https://regent.edu/journal/journal-of-virtues-leadership/character-and-servant-leadership-ten-characteristics-of-effective-caring-leaders on January 2, 2023.

Statistics Canada. (2017, March 8). *Study: Women in Canada—Women and paid work.* Accessed at https://www150.statcan.gc.ca/n1/daily-quotidien/170308/dq170308b-eng.htm?HPA=1 on January 2, 2023.

Stone, A. G., Russell, R. F., & Patterson, K. (2003, August). *Transformational versus servant leadership: A difference in leader focus.* Accessed at https://regent.edu/wp-content/uploads/2020/12/stone_transformation_versus.pdf on October 18, 2022.

Stuck, A. M, & Byars, L. (2022, May 11) *Relational aggression: Definition, types, & impacts.* Accessed at https://choosingtherapy.com/relational-aggression on October 18, 2022.

Substance Abuse and Mental Health Services Administration. (2014). *A treatment improvement protocol: Trauma-informed care in behavioral health services—Tip 57.* Rockville, MD: U.S. Department of Health and Human Services. Accessed at https://store.samhsa.gov/sites/default/files/d7/priv/sma14-4816.pdf on January 23, 2023.

Sutcher, L., Darling-Hammond, L., & Carver-Thomas, D. (2016, September 15). *A coming crisis in teaching? Teacher supply, demand, and shortages in the U.S.* Palo Alto, CA: Learning Policy Institute. Accessed at https://learningpolicyinstitute.org/product/coming-crisis-teaching on June 19, 2021.

Syntrio. (2021, August 10). *The negative impact of gossip in the workplace* [Blog post]. Accessed at https://syntrio.com/blog/the-negative-impact-of-gossip-in-the-workplace on October 18, 2022.

Tait, B. (2020, March 11). *Traditional leadership vs. servant leadership.* Accessed at https://forbes.com/sites/forbescoachescouncil/2020/03/11/traditional-leadership-vs-servant-leadership/?sh=1f383f26451e on January 2, 2023.

Tanner, L. (2020, March 7). *Creating a SWOT analysis—On your own leadership skills and abilities.* Accessed at http://middlemanaged.com/2020/03/07/creating-a-swot-analysis-on-your-own-leadership-skills-and-abilities on January 3, 2023.

Taylor, J. (2020, August 12). *Self-care: What it is and what it is not.* Accessed at https://news.dasa.ncsu.edu/self-care-what-it-is-and-what-it-is-not on October 18, 2022.

Theisen, A. (2021, December 8). *Is a sense of belonging important?* Accessed at https://mayoclinichealthsystem.org/hometown-health/speaking-of-health/is-having-a-sense-of-belonging-important on October 18, 2022.

Tiny Buddha. (n.d.). *A lot of what weighs you down isn't yours to carry.* Accessed at https://tinybuddha.com/wisdom-quotes/a-lot-of-what-weighs-you-down-isnt-yours-to-carry on January 19, 2023.

Trauma. (n.d.). In *Oxford Learner's Dictionaries online.* Accessed at https://oxfordlearnersdictionaries.com/definition/english/trauma on January 23, 2023.

Trauma Dissociation.com. (n.d.). *History of PTSD and trauma diagnoses*. Accessed at http://traumadissociation.com/ptsd/history-of-post-traumatic-stress-disorder.html on February 9, 2022.

Trauma-Informed Care for Children and Families Act. (2017). *Bill summary*. Accessed at https://billtrack50.com/BillDetail/865793 on January 2, 2023.

Trauma Informed Oregon. (n.d.). *Homepage*. Accessed at https://traumainformedoregon.org on October 18, 2022.

Trauma Informed Oregon. (2014). *Guiding principles of trauma informed care: SAMHSA's concept of trauma and guidance for a trauma-informed care approach* [Infographic]. Accessed at https://traumainformedoregon.org/wp-content/uploads/2020/02/Principles-of-Trauma-Informed-Care.pdf on October 4, 2021.

Tyler, R. (2020, April 22). *How to reduce stress and to improve your executive functioning*. Accessed at https://connectionsinmind.com/stress_executivefunctions on February 25, 2022.

Tyndale House Publishers. (1996). *Life application study Bible NLT*. Carol Stream, IL: Author.

Unannotated New Mexico Statutes. (n.d.). *Chapter 74: Environmental improvement—Article 12, Night sky protection*. Accessed at http://darkskynm.org/nspa.pdf on January 23, 2023.

University of Buffalo. (n.d.). *What is trauma-informed care?* Buffalo, NY: Buffalo Center for Social Research. Accessed at http://socialwork.buffalo.edu/social-research/institutes-centers/institute-on-trauma-and-trauma-informed-care/what-is-trauma-informed-care.html on October 20, 2021.

Unyte Integrated Listening Systems. (2018, September 13). *What is trauma?* Accessed at https://integratedlistening.com/what-is-trauma on October 21, 2021.

U.S. Department of Education. (n.d.). *ED school climate surveys: Instructional staff survey*. Accessed at https://nces.ed.gov/surveys/edscls/pdf/EDSCLS_Instructional_Questionnaire.pdf on Febraury 20, 2023.

U.S. News Education. (n.d.). *Best middle schools: Paradise Charter Middle School*. Accessed at https://usnews.com/education/k12/california/paradise-charter-middle-266931 on April 6, 2022.

U.S. Travel Association. (2019, August 16). *Study: A record 768 million U.S. vacation days went unused in '18, opportunity cost in the billions* [Press release]. Accessed at https://ustravel.org/press/study-record-768-million-us-vacation-days-went-unused-18-opportunity-cost-billions on October 18, 2022.

Utah State Board of Education. (2020, March). *Strategies for personal self-care* [Infographic]. Accessed at https://schools.utah.gov/file/dc16ab51-3c3d-44d8-ba8b-8c05fe330a33 on October 18, 2022.

Villines, Z. (2019, June 6). *Disordered executive function: What to know*. Accessed at https://medicalnewstoday.com/articles/325402 on February 25, 2022.

Walker, T. (2018, May 11). *How many teachers are highly stressed? Maybe more than people think*. Accessed at https://nea.org/advocating-for-change/new-from-nea/how-many-teachers-are-highly-stressed-maybe-more-people-think on October 18, 2022.

Walker, T. (2019, October 18). *"I didn't know it had a name": Secondary traumatic stress and educators.* Accesses at https://nea.org/advocating-for-change/new-from-nea/i-didnt-know-it-had-name-secondary-traumatic-stress-and on December 30, 2022.

Walker, T. (2022, February 1). *Survey: Alarming number of educators may soon leave the profession.* Accessed at https://nea.org/advocating-for-change/new-from-nea/survey-alarming-number-educators-may-soon-leave-profession on October 18, 2022.

Wilkinson, D. (n.d.). *The difference between organizational culture and climate and why it matters* [Blog post]. Accessed at https://oxford-review.com/blog-research-difference-culture-climate/#:~:text=The%20organisational%20climate%20on%20the,day%20basis%20or%20just%20generally on January 24, 2023.

World Health Organization. (2019, April 2). *Self-care can be an effective part of national health systems.* Accessed at https://who.int/news/item/02-04-2019-self-care-can-be-an-effective-part-of-national-health-systems on January 25, 2023.

World Health Organization. (2019, May 28). *Burn-out an "occupational phenomenon": International Classification of Diseases.* Accessed at https://who.int/news/item/28-05-2019-burn-out-an-occupational-phenomenon-international-classification-of-diseases on October 17, 2022.

Zubrzycki, J. (2015, December 18). Year-round schooling explained. *Education Week.* Accessed at https://edweek.org/leadership/year-round-schooling-explained/2015/12 on January 3, 2023.

Index

A
active listening, 61
acute stress, 28. *See also stress*
acute trauma, 24. See also trauma
adverse childhood experiences (ACEs)
    about, 23–24
    and choice, 83
    leadership ACEs survey reproducible, 38–39
    rate of, 25, 121
    and think time and processing time, 81–82
    and trauma-informed care, 43–44
agenda planner reproducible, 93
American Psychiatric Association, 23

B
Ballard, D., 105–106
behaviors, functional versus dysfunctional work family behaviors, 50
being present
    actions to prevent burnout, 27
    team leadership and, 77
beliefs
    elements of organizational culture, 14
    impact of, 10
    norms and, 13
Blanchard, K., 61
Brown, B., 79
bullying
    chronic trauma and, 24
    identifying toxicity within an organization, 98
    relational aggression and, 50, 84
    toxic stress and, 6
burnout
    actions to prevent burnout, 27–28
    benches in the bathroom and, 1–4
    burnout risk scale reproducible, 36–37
    compassion fatigue and toxic stress and, 30–31
    connections and, 75
    definition of, 30
    hiring for zeal and, 102
    impact of, 9
    respecting time away and, 86, 87
    school calendar and, 107
    teacher attrition and, 9
    transformational and servant leadership and, 65
    vacations and, 105–106
Burns, J., 64

C

CDC's six guiding principles to trauma-informed practices, 44–45
celebrations
    connections and, 49
    reproducibles for, 55
    wellness initiatives and, 110
ceremonies. *See rituals and ceremonies*
change, fear of, 96–97
check and connect strategy, 76
checking in first, 77–79
chronic trauma, 24, 26. See also trauma
climate surveys, 11–12
community
    servant leadership and, 63
    team leadership and, 80–81
compassion, definition of, 47
compassion fatigue
    burnout and toxic stress and, 30–31
    connection and, 75
    stress and, 3
    transformational and servant leadership and, 65
complex trauma, 24–25, 26. *See also trauma*
conceptualization, 63–64
connections
    building community and, 80
    organization as family and, 49
    team leadership and, 75–76
culture
    organizational strategies for changing culture, 97
    organizational culture. *See organizational culture*
    school culture. *See school culture*
cultures of wellness. *See also wellness*
    about, 9–10
    culture within, 18–20
    elements of organizational culture in your school, 11–15
    framework for, 17
    framework for, people-first leadership and, 65–67
    framework for, trauma-compassionate approach and, 47–48
    hiring into a culture of, 127–128
    impact of organizational climate and culture, 10–11
    maintaining and replicating, 128–130
    what a well school culture is, 16–17
    what a well school culture is not, 15–16

D

Diagnostic and Statistical Manual of Mental Disorders (American Psychiatric Association), 23
dress code, 12

E

emotional safety, 83–86
empathy, 61–62
eustress, 28. *See also stress*
executive functioning, 31–32

F

Faith, B., 122–123, 124–125
family
    functional versus dysfunctional work family behaviors, 50
    organization as family, 48–50
fear of change, 96–97
fight-flight-freeze-fawn responses, 25–26
Ford, E., picture of mother and, 136
foresight, 63
four I's of transformational leadership, 64–65
framework for a culture of wellness. *See also cultures of wellness*
    about, 17
    people-first leadership and, 65–67
    trauma-compassionate approach and, 47–48

Friedman, M., 23, 25

G
gossip, 85, 98
Greater Good Magazine, 47
Greenleaf, R., 60–61, 62
growth
    maintaining culture in the face of, 126–127
    servant leadership and, 63

H
healing, 62
hiring
    hiring for zeal, 102–104, 115–116
    hiring into a culture of wellness, 127–128
    think time and processing time and, 82
human experience, creating space for, 100–102

I
iCan Dream Center
    about, 3–4
    emotional safety and, 85
    hiring for zeal and, 102
    including wellness in collective bargaining, 107
    maintaining and replicating a culture of wellness and, 129
    paying it forward and, 88
    rituals and ceremonies at, 14
    think time and, 82
    values at, 14, 49, 81
idealized influence, 65
impulse control, 32
individualized consideration, 65
infusing choice, 83
inspirational motivation, 65
intellectual stimulation, 65
intrinsic motivation, 87
introduction
    about benches in the bathroom and burnout, 1–4
    about this book, 5–7
isolation of targets, 85–86

J
journey to wellness. *See also Paradise Charter Middle School (PCMS); wellness*
    about, 119–120
    culture within, 131–133
    strategies for cultural wellness at Paradise, 123–130
    working and learning in Paradise, 120–123

K
Kenzie Academy, 80

L
leadership. *See also organizational leadership; people-first leadership; team leadership*
    leadership ACEs survey reproducible, 38–39
    servant leadership, 60–64
    transformational leadership, 64–65
    trauma-informed care and its contribution to effective leadership, 42–46
    universal design approach and, 4
Leadership (Burns), 64
Lewis, M., 96
listening
    actions to prevent burnout, 28
    servant leadership and, 61

M
Maslow's hierarchy of needs, 100–101
meetings, 79–80, 93
Merriam-Webster, 30
microaggressions, 29
modeling

actions to prevent burnout, 28
modeling self-care as a critical action in leading a physically, emotionally, and socially safe school culture, 137

N

norms, 13–14

O

organizational strategies for changing culture, 97
organizational culture
    definition of, 10
    elements of organizational culture, 11–15
    identifying toxicity within an organization, 98–100
    impact of organizational climate and culture, 10–11
    servant leadership and, 61
    what a well school culture is, 16–17
    what a well school culture is not, 15–16
organizational leadership. *See also leadership*
    about, 95–96
    creating space for the human experience, 100–102
    culture within, 112–114
    encouraging vacations, 104–107
    fear of change and, 96–97
    giving staff permission to engage in self-care, 109–111
    hiring for zeal, 102–104
    identifying toxicity within an organization, 98–100
    including wellness in collective bargaining, 107–108
    reproducibles for, 115–117

P

pain points
    about, 21–23
    culture within, 33–35
    foundational knowledge about trauma, 23–28
    reproducibles for, 36–39
    toxic stress as a form of trauma, 28–32
Paradise Charter Middle School (PCMS). *See also journey to wellness*
    cultivating passion, 124–126
    hiring into a culture of wellness, 127–128
    maintaining and replicating a culture of wellness, 128–130
    maintaining culture in the face of growth, 126–127
    strategies for cultural wellness at Paradise, 123–130
    strengths-based approach, 123–124
    working and learning in Paradise, 120–123
passion, cultivating, 124–126
people-first leadership. *See also leadership*
    about, 16–17, 57–59
    culture within, 68–70
    framework for a culture of wellness and, 17, 65–67
    philosophies of, 59–65
    reproducibles for, 71
persuasion, 62
Peterson, K., 11
physical abuse, 21
physical trauma, 23. *See also trauma*
positive stress, 28. *See also stress*
post-traumatic stress disorder (PTSD), 23, 25
processing time, 81–83
psychological trauma, 23, 24, 25. See also trauma

R

RACI board reproducible, 94
racism and toxic stress, 29

reflection, 27
Reid, C., 123, 128
relational aggression
    bullying and, 50
    guarding emotional safety and, 84–85
    isolation of targets and, 85
    toxic stress and, 29
reproducibles for
    burnout risk scale, 36–37
    hiring for zeal, 115–116
    leadership ACEs survey, 38–39
    meeting agenda planner, 93
    RACI board, 94
    SWOP analysis, 71
    traditions and celebrations planning tool, 55
    wellness initiative planning checklist, 117
respecting time away
    encouraging vacations and, 104–107
    team leadership and, 86–87
rituals and ceremonies
    connections and, 49
    elements of organizational culture, 14
    identifying toxicity within an organization, 99
    norms and, 13
    reproducibles for, 55

S

safe space, 119, 120
school breaks, 107–108
school calendar/including wellness in collective bargaining, 107–108
school culture. *See also organizational culture*
    definition of, 11
    what a well school culture is, 16–17
    what a well school culture is not, 15–16
secondary traumatic stress, 27. *See also vicarious trauma*
self-awareness
    actions to prevent burnout, 27
    checking in first, 78
    foresight and, 63
    philosophies of people-first leadership and, 59
    servant leadership and, 62
self-care
    author's experience with, 135–136
    giving staff permission to engage in, 109–111
    modeling self-care as a critical action in leading a physically, emotionally, and socially safe school culture, 137
Seppällä, E., 105
servant leadership, 60–64. *See also leadership*
sexual harassment, 30
Society for Human Resource Management, 10
soft skills, 102–103
span of control, 129
stewardship, 62
Stone, A., 65
stories and symbols, 14–15
strengths-based approach, 123–124
stress. *See also toxic stress*
    actions to prevent burnout from, 27–28
    educators and, 1–3
    fear of change and, 96
    impact of, 15
    responses to traumatic stressors, 25–26
structure, creating, 79–80
summer slide, 107–108
surveys, anonymous climate surveys, 11–12
SWOP analysis, 66, 71

T

teachers
    teacher attrition, 2, 3, 5
    vicarious trauma and its connection to teachers, 26–28

team leadership. *See also* leadership
    about, 73–75
    being present, 77
    building community, 80–81
    checking in first, 77–79
    creating connection, 75–76
    creating structure, 79–80
    culture within, 90–92
    emotional safety and, 83–86
    infusing choice, 83
    paying it forward, 87–89
    reproducibles for, 93–94
    respecting time away, 86–87
    utilizing think time and processing time, 81–83
team players, three virtues of, 103
team-level strategies for changing culture, 97
teams, definition of, 74
think time, 81–83
tolerable stress, 28. *See also* stress
toxic culture, 15
toxic stress. *See also* stress
    about, 28–29
    burnout and compassion fatigue and, 30–31
    definition of, 28
    executive functioning and, 31–32
    how toxic stress finds its way into the workplace, 29
    sources of at work, 29–30
toxicity, identifying within an organization, 98–100
traditions and celebrations, reproducibles for, 55
transformational leadership, 64–65. *See also leadership*
trauma
    categories of, 22
    definition of, 23
    educators and, 1–2
    foundational knowledge about trauma, 23–28
    impact of, 22
    loss of control and infusing choice, 83
    responses to traumatic stressors, 25–26
    subtypes of, 24–25
    toxic stress as a form of, 28–32
    types of, 23
    vicarious trauma and its connection to teachers, 26–28
trauma-informed care
    about, 42–43
    CDC's six guiding principles to, 44–45
    checking in first and, 77–78
    education and, 43–44
    in practice, 45–46
    trauma compassionate and, 47
trauma-informed compassion
    about, 16, 41–42
    culture within, 52–54
    framework for a culture of wellness and, 17, 47–48
    organization as family and, 48–51
    reproducibles for, 55
    from trauma informed to trauma compassionate, 47
    trauma-informed care and its contribution to effective leadership. *See trauma-informed care*
triggers. *See pain points*

U

universal design approach, 4

V

vacations
    encouraging vacations, 104–107
    including wellness in collective bargaining, 107–108
    respecting time away, 86–87
values

elements of organizational culture, 14
at iCan Dream Center, 14, 49, 81
impact of, 10
norms and, 13
vicarious trauma, 26–28. *See also trauma*
vision
four I's of transformational leadership and, 64–65
maintaining culture in the face of growth, 126, 127

W

wellness. *See also cultures of wellness; journey to wellness*
including wellness in collective bargaining, 107–108
reproducibles for, 117
wellness initiatives
planning for, 110–111
reproducibles for, 117
work expectations
elements of organizational culture, 12–13
overwork and, 2
toxic stress and, 29
work relationships. *See also community*
creating space for the human experience and, 101
organization as family and, 48–50
World Health Organization, 30

Beyond Self-Care
Gail Markin
Explore the importance of well-being at individual, group, and system levels, as well as the role of leadership in supporting school cultures of well-being. Using research-based practices and excerpts of conversations from working educators, Markin delivers a guidebook to healthier, more passionate schools.
BKG079

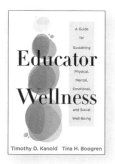

Educator Wellness
Timothy D. Kanold and Tina H. Boogren
How do we bring our best selves to our students and colleagues each day? Designed as a reflective journal and guidebook, *Educator Wellness* will take you on a deep exploration where you will uncover profound answers that ring true for you.
BKG053

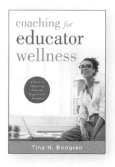

Coaching for Educator Wellness
Tina H. Boogren
Acquire evergreen coaching strategies alongside fresh new solutions for differentiating support for new and veteran teachers, addressing teacher self-care, and more. You'll turn to this resource again and again as you continue to improve your craft and help teachers find their own greatness.
BKF989

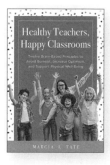

Healthy Teachers, Happy Classrooms
Marcia L. Tate
Best-selling author Marcia L. Tate delivers 12 principles proven by brain research to help you thrive personally and professionally. Each chapter digs into the benefits of these self-care strategies and offers suggestions for bringing the practice to life in your classroom.
BKG044

Visit SolutionTree.com or call 800.733.6786 to order.

GLOBAL PD

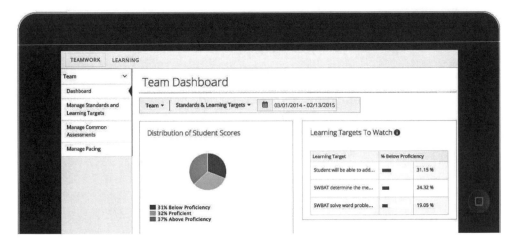

The **Power to Improve**
Is in Your Hands

Global PD gives educators focused and goals-oriented training from top experts. You can rely on this innovative online tool to improve instruction in every classroom.

- Get unlimited, on-demand access to guided video and book content from top Solution Tree authors.

- Improve practices with personalized virtual coaching from PLC-certified trainers.

- Customize learning based on skill level and time commitments.

▶ **REQUEST A FREE DEMO TODAY**
SolutionTree.com/GlobalPD